W9-BFZ-084

putting
the
GIANTS
to sleep

Cover art: "Fearless," by Jim Warren ©1991
Cover design by Pam Norpell

stories and exercises
for awakening self-worth

David Sheinkin, M.D.

Edited by Edward Hoffman, Ph.D.

This publication made possible with
the assistance of the Kern Foundation

Wheaton, Ill. U.S.A.
Madras, India/London, England

The Theosophical Publishing House
P.O. Box 270
Wheaton, IL 60189-0270

A publication of the Theosophical Publishing House,
a department of the Theosophical Society in America

**Library of Congress Cataloging-in Publication Data**

Sheinkin, David, 1939–1982
Putting the giants to sleep : stories and exercises for awakening self-worth / David Sheinkin : edited by Edward Hoffman.
p. cm.
"Quest books."
Includes bibliographical references.
ISBN 0-8356-0673-2 (pbk.) : $11.95
1. Conduct of life. 2. Mind and body. 3. Meditation.
4. Self-esteem — Problems, exercises, etc. I. Hoffman, Edward, 1951- . II. Title.
BF637.C5S54 1991
158'.1 — dc20 91-50275
CIP

Printed in the United States of America

If I am not for myself, who will be?
If I am only for myself, what am I?
If not now, when?

Hillel the Elder
*Pirke Avoth*

# Contents

# Foreword

## The David Sheinkin Memorial Fellowship

*We are driven by an awareness that something is asked of us, that we are asked to wonder, to revere, to think and to love in a way that is compatible with the grandeur and mystery of living.*

Abraham Heschel,
*Between God and Man*

David was a gifted teacher and therapist. His exceptional intelligence and insight enabled him to integrate the traditional and the non-traditional, and to make complex teachings vital and meaningful for the rest of us. David's ability to perceive truths within everyday experiences, combined with a gentle sense of humor, made him a master storyteller.

To David, a ride to the circus with a car full of restless children became a metaphor for life itself. His non-judgmental acceptance of himself and others created an atmosphere in which we came to know ourselves better and by extension, to envision meaning beyond ourselves. The material presented in this book reflects both David's journey in search of personal truth and his ongoing commitment to healing others.

Because of our love for him and our recognition of

his uniqueness, we have created the David Sheinkin Memorial Fellowship. As part of our mission, we are helping to publish his work posthumously. David taught us ways to explore life's mysteries with joy and reverence, and we feel privileged to have shared his insight, his delight, his humor, and his wisdom.

# Editor's Note

Edward Hoffman, Ph.D.

Having had the privilege of editing David Sheinkin's manuscript on the Kabbalah a few years ago, I marvel once more at his ability to impart teachings from the world's great spiritual traditions in such a clear and concise manner. He had a truly unique talent in this regard, for which his many students and colleagues continue to remember him with affectionate admiration. For this second book, Dr. Sheinkin's intent was to draw upon these age-old systems of knowledge for their practical relevance in helping us all to enhance our self-worth, and thereby live more joyfully and productively.

In producing this volume for the David Sheinkin Memorial Fellowship, I have been faced with the challenge of combining and editing an unfinished manuscript and a series of diverse transcribed lectures. Perhaps inevitably, I have been obliged to condense or omit tantalizing material not sufficiently developed to have blended well with the overall theme of this work. Had he lived longer, Dr. Sheinkin would have further shared his insights with us on such matters, I am certain. But from the wealth of ideas and techniques on improving self-worth that he presented in this book, I feel equally sure that his goals for it would have been fulfilled, and I am grateful for the opportunity to have helped make that possible.

# Preface

Not long ago, I became convinced that most people who grow up in our culture lack a strong sense of self-worth, and consequently, experience needless unhappiness and emotional pain. As a psychiatrist committed to a holistic approach, I set out to help reverse this situation. After working with hundreds of persons during the past few years, I decided to write this book as a way to share the methods that I have found to be relevant and effective.

From the outset, I wish to emphasize that I do not claim to have discovered any startling truths. On the contrary, I have learned that the most potent means of strengthening a positive sense of self have been known and practiced for centuries. I have also learned that most individuals need to hear certain truths repeated many times before fully absorbing them. This book is intended to be one of those times. It offers practical methods to call forth and encourage the growth of our self-worth. Though we each must find our own way in life, our journey may be considerably enhanced if we follow proven and time-honored guideposts.

In my own endeavors, I have been fortunate to have studied with masters of several disciplines described in the pages that follow. But ironically, I have often gained more from encounters with their students. This situation was especially true when I began my search for ways to enhance self-worth—when the gulf between the master and myself seemed immense. I could only marvel at some of my teachers, who radiated such grace and artistry. But I could more meaningfully observe their students, closer to my own fledgling efforts. Yet, I believe, to enhance self-worth, we need not truly master any of the techniques described in this volume. Rather, such efforts are aspects of a never-ending process, and not a specific, goal-oriented activity. Consequently, the benefits you may gain from this book come, above all, from being involved in the process.

In *Illusions*, Richard Bach writes, "You teach best what you most need to learn." This observation is certainly true for me, and has undoubtedly been my primary motivation for writing this book.

# Introduction

My story begins one day when I was in high school and had to write one of those inane compositions we all remember. The topic was something similar to "What I did on my summer vacation." Only this assignment was in the middle of the school year, so our class was asked to write on "What I want to be when I grow up."

I recall writing about wanting to be a psychiatrist. But what happened was that I mispelled the word "psychiatrist," and the teacher let me know this before the whole class. She also pointed out that this profession was probably something I wouldn't want to pursue, because otherwise, I would know how to spell it. She questioned me about what a psychiatrist does, and it rapidly became clear that I hadn't the vaguest idea. My teacher seemed correct in her judgment.

I couldn't spell the word "psychiatrist," and I couldn't really define it either. But somehow I still knew that I wanted to be a psychiatrist. Because I didn't know the requirements, I obtained a long list of them: completion of high school and college, then medical school, internship, and so on. My response was, "Okay, if that's what I have to do, I'll do it." It made no difference what was on the list. I was prepared to do it all.

And so, I set about to accomplish those things, never questioning them. I kept my goal in mind all through college and medical school. I purposely avoided psychology courses and took no electives in psychiatry, since I was so sure that this would be my eventual profession. I devoted my time to learning other subjects, including anatomy and physiology, the nature of the human body. I also became interested in the whole concept of health and illness.

But by the time I finished medical school, I was convinced that something was missing—what we had learned was correct, but something had been omitted. I was sure that the key to human existence lay not in the body, but somewhere in the mind. In a way, this had been my conviction since high school: I knew I would have to explore the human mind to understand what life was all about.

After my internship, which I regarded as my last hurdle, I began psychiatric residency. At that time, I was interested in a Freudian approach to the field. After three years of residency and a couple of years of psychoanalytic institute training, I thought that I had really gained mastery. I felt I understood myself and others.

Then life interfered. During the Vietnam War, I was drafted into the U. S. Air Force and stationed in Mississippi. Military service marked my first major break from a life spent mainly in school and university settings, where everyone shared similar beliefs. Within that framework, my training and ideas had worked rather nicely, it seemed.

But in Mississippi, I was far from a university setting and in the midst of a population needing immediate answers to pressing problems, not long-term approaches like psychoanalysis. I realized that everything

I had studied and worked for until then had very little relevance in this world. For example, a sergeant was having emotional problems, and I naively said, "Okay, let's meet twice a week for the next year-and-a-half." He laughed in reply. Frightened young airmen would say, "Doctor, I'm going to be shipped to Vietnam in two weeks. What am I going to do?" I had little to offer.

My first reaction was, "How stupid this Air Force system is! What is our country coming to?" I was convinced that I was right and that everyone around me was wrong. I was prepared to give the Air Force chief a list of suggestions on how to improve the system. But I was able to fool myself with that outlook for only a short while. Soon I became depressed when I realized that despite all my academic preparation, I was not prepared for this very real situation.

I faced two choices. The first was to enjoy Air Force life, which in fact made few demands on me, and do very little within the existing system. Everyone would have been content with this choice except me. The other choice was to look for answers outside my formal education. I had studied hypnosis and behavior modification a bit. I knew that there were approaches besides psychoanalysis, but I hadn't valued these techniques. I had always relegated them to a rather lowly position.

In my frustration, I decided to examine these other approaches with interest. My need to find alternative methods led me to humanistic approaches, such as Gestalt psychology, Gestalt therapy, and Reichian body therapy, for example. My emphasis shifted from an intellectual understanding of human feeling to an approach that emphasized its direct experience. This was a whole new direction for me. My pursuit opened many doors in me, and I began to offer others greater help, too. For several years, I experienced exciting growth.

Then I arrived at another plateau. Each time I thought I had added the missing ingredient of understanding, I would benefit from it and be grateful. But I would still conclude that there was something missing.

The next step I took was toward parapsychology. In this field, people seemed to be talking about something different from what I had known. I did extensive study and traveled to several countries to meet with leaders in the parapsychology field, who were doing serious work. I concluded that they were touching something important, but their work wasn't what I was seeking.

What was I seeking? In retrospect, the answer is clear. There was another aspect to myself—and to everybody—our spirituality. Yet nobody in my background had ever addressed this facet of our existence—not in medical school, not in psychoanalytic training, not in humanistic psychology. As that awareness slowly dawned, my need to explore the spiritual dimensions of life grew. I realized that to find my answers I needed to explore this dimension too.

To a certain extent, that is what I have been doing for nearly the last decade. I believe now that the answer I was seeking doesn't lie in the spiritual dimension any more than it lies wholly in the physical or mental aspects of life. I now regard all these factors as essential parts of our being that we need to integrate. If we focus too much on one as opposed to the others, then no matter how much we develop, we will feel out of kilter.

The most important issue for me is developing balance, both in myself and in others. I find that the best way to develop balance within is through sharing the process. I want to be open about that. The main reason

I share anything with people is because that's the way I learn it and perfect it within myself. But part of the issue is also how to make the subject practical. Why? Because people can give many sermons about self-integration, and it can all be very abstract. Indeed, the reason that I had never been much interested in searching for truth within religion was probably because of its abstractions: I had been looking for practical answers, not sermons.

Can the spiritual traditions, then, be made so practical that we can benefit from them right at the outset? Can I help you to experience what I say as true? Otherwise, my words are just abstractions without much meaning or relevance. Motivated by this question, I have studied many spiritual systems, just as I had previously studied many medical and psychological systems. My goal throughout has been to determine if it's possible to glean practical advice that can be shared with others. That goal is what this book is about.

What specifically does this book cover? I must preface my remarks by stressing that it's not possible to discuss our physical, emotional, and spiritual aspects at the same time. Language forces us to address one or another. Each of these three realms, of course, can be divided into many subcategories. We will have to address them separately, but our ultimate aim is to integrate them, to bring these elements together in our lives.

*It is my belief that the essence of a person lies in the appropriate balance of body, mind, and spirit, and that self-worth derives from the awareness of a connection to this balance and its independence from outside approval, accomplishment, or acquisition.*

To this end, I wish to focus on how we can tap into the power that resides within the mind. We know from biofeedback and other medical studies that the human mind can control virtually every bodily function, such as temperature, blood pressure, and muscular tension. Within the mind is tremendous power to affect every aspect of our bodies. Yet, most of us lack even the vaguest notion of how to tap into this power. I'd like to introduce the idea that it is possible through simple exercises to develop an awareness of your possibilities in this domain. By doing so, you will gain entry into a whole area of power within yourself.

I explain basic relaxation methods designed to create the stillness necessary for many inward states. I also address the realm of emotions, particularly the negative experiences of anger, fear, and envy. Our feeling life is profoundly affected by our attitudes, so I discuss how emotions interact and what we can do to create positive feelings in place of negative ones.

A key facet of spiritual growth that I discuss in this book is meditation. I do so first, because meditation is the foundation for our spiritual development, and second, because there is considerable confusion about meditation. Many people have spent years meditating without becoming more balanced than they were at the beginning of their practice, except that perhaps they know how to relax better. But meditation is not just another method for relaxation.

What kind of tool is meditation? What can we accomplish with it? What are its dangers? I've heard over and over about wondrous gains from meditation, and almost never about its potentially destructive aspects. There is nothing in this universe that can be used only for good. Every source of power can be used for either good or evil, growth or destruction. Whether we speak about nuclear energy or meditation, unless we are cognizant of the power involved, we are likely to overlook the danger. So I am clear about some of meditation's dangers and early warning signs.

I also talk about experiencing daily events from a spiritual perspective. That is, what do the great traditions teach about our everyday problems and concerns? What do they say about the fields of energy that reside within us waiting to be tapped?

Of course, whether we focus on spiritual or psychological issues, we must do our work within our embodied form. How we relate to our bodies affects all the work we do. Therefore, I will discuss issues that impact on our physical well-being, such as nutrition and exercise. Even how we breathe is important to examine. So seemingly simple, breathing is an integrating force that encompasses mind, body, and spirit. As long as we are going to breathe anyway, we may as well learn to do it effectively and powerfully.

You will probably not become expert in any of these methods by reading this book. Rather, my hope is to offer you methods that can serve as an introduction to ideas and techniques that you can pursue in greater depth. If you do, be aware that all require hard work and discipline. Indeed, the key word for them all is *discipline*, a skill involving time, more difficult for many of us to obtain today than money. So, know beforehand that we examine areas like meditation that are time-consuming and that involve hard work and discipline. You may wonder whether you'll find the time for these activities, and I hope to give you direction on that issue as well.

All these methods work, and for some people, they work remarkably well. The most important thing is to see which techniques work best for you, and to stick with these faithfully. The result can be to make your life more meaningful and satisfying in every way.

# 1

# Finding Balance in an Unbalanced World

*I spoke to him about the emptiness. . . . Sometimes, not too often anymore, that old pain returns. It's a longing, an aloneness, an opening in my chest that aches to be filled. I cope by accepting its presence and by knowing that it will pass. I cry, I smoke a cigarette, I withdraw into myself and my music and dreams. I do not expect reality to satisfy my longing, but rather, to gradually muffle its voice.*

*And reality meets my expectations—for a while.*

*"Why not fill the emptiness?" he asked one day.*

*"Idiot!" I thought.*

*I said, "I can't be daddy's little girl anymore—I can't touch my mother's soft cheek!"*

*His message was: "There are new relationships to fill old needs," and I struggled with that message for days afterward. In fact, I had those new relationships. I had a husband far more loving than anyone else in my life had been. I loved the warmth of his body, the magic of his mind, the beauty of his spirit. I loved him, and yet my emptiness remained. I had three children, each a gift of God: beautiful, caring, responsive, growing. I loved them and yet my emptiness remained.*

*Why? Something was lacking, some ingredient that would allow me to feel nurtured from these nurturing bonds. The love to fill my longing was present. But my capacity to connect with that love, to feel its comfort and nourishment deep within my being was missing, or damaged, or hidden.*

M.G.

After seven years of practicing psychiatry exclusively, my interest in treating the whole person led me to expand my practice to general medicine as well. For the past five years I have practiced both disciplines. Quite unexpectedly after undertaking this expansion, I noticed that nearly all my patients, regardless of their symptoms or specific requests for help, shared a common difficulty: All were lacking in their sense of self-worth.

Initially, this observation made little impact on me. After all, it seemed obvious that psychiatric patients would lack self-worth. What was so noteworthy about that? But after I began treating patients who suffered from a wide variety of chronic and degenerative diseases, I realized that nearly every individual seeking medical help shared this same basic deficit. Undoubtedly, my background in psychiatry affected the way I related to patients and enabled me to see people and not merely their symptoms.

How is it that they are all lacking in self-worth? I kept asking myself. However, it wasn't until I changed the nature of my question that I began to get an answer. After puzzling over the low self-worth of people who were seriously ill, I took a better look at my friends and relatives, and at myself as well. I found that most of us had the same difficulty. After confirming and reconfirming this basic observation, my question changed to: How can *we all* be lacking in self-worth?

Gradually, I came to see that the answer lay not in

any one factor or experience, but rather in the very fabric of our culture. Our culture begins influencing us even before we are born and leaves its mark on every subsequent phase of our development.

## WHAT IS SELF-WORTH?

Webster defines "self" as "the essential qualities of any person or thing," and "worth" as "importance, value, merit." The definition of "self-worth" inevitably varies from culture to culture—and even among individuals within a specific culture—depending chiefly on what the culture regards as our individual essence. But in my view, these varying definitions pertain more to "self-esteem" and "self-image" than to "self-worth."

For example, if a culture prizes prowess in sports, then outstanding athletes are likely to be venerated by large numbers of people. Such athletes may develop high self-esteem, a judgment of themselves based on an arbitrary definition of merit. *But they may still feel disconnected from meaningful parts of themselves and thus lack what I am calling self-worth.* The prevalence of alcohol or drug dependency among wealthy, successful athletes illustrates this point clearly. Likewise, self-image involves comparing ourselves to some arbitrary standard of what we should be like. Satisfying this cultural criterion can give us a positive self-image, but it will not boost our inner sense of self.

Of course, there are no real boundaries between body, mind and spirit. We are one total organism. But to master any integrated activity—from swinging a tennis racket, to performing a ballet, driving a car, or flying an airplane—we must learn the integration step-by-step, dealing at different times with different aspects, until they flow together as a whole. The same is true for understanding the integration of body, mind, and spirit that makes up a human being. Focusing on any one aspect of our being is not necessarily a negation of the whole. Indeed, it is often a necessary step in grasping that totality. However, ignoring or disowning any element of our being is surely a negation of our wholeness.

Others may insist that the body-mind has little to do with our essence, for they see our true self as only spiritual. However, we remain living human creatures only so long as we have a body-mind, even if there is a spiritual part of ourselves capable of existence independent of our body-mind.

Still others may contend that there is no need to put forward nonexistent or nonproven spiritual factors to explain our day-to-day behavior or self-worth. This is true enough, for I don't regard the word "spiritual" as crucial to understanding ourselves. But I use the word because I believe that there is a part of us which is *beyond* our concept of body-mind. While it may be possible to explain all spiritual phenomena as experiences of the body-mind, to do so necessitates expanding the definitions of mind and body far beyond their common usages. In addition, scientists have hardly discovered all the aspects of our body-mind, and what our culture sometimes terms "spiritual" may be only a reflection of current scientific ignorance. Therefore, we can choose to think of the transcendent aspect of ourselves as truly *beyond* body-mind, or decide that this *beyond* refers simply to portions of our being not yet understood by orthodox science.

Whatever the semantics, it seems clear from everyday experience that developing and caring for our body may improve our self-image, but will not necessarily enhance our self-worth. Neither will possessing a high IQ or having ready access to our emotions always be synonymous with increased self-worth. Even in combination, these factors may bring us greater self-esteem but fall short of influencing our fundamental self-worth. True self-worth requires something more—not a replacement, but an addition. I call this additional ingredient, "the spiritual connection."

Before I completed the manuscript for this book, I met with my original editor. We spent a pleasant evening together and discussed many subjects, some related to the book in progress. At one point, in talking about the many cultural determinants that hinder self-worth, I cited the current widespread devaluing of spirituality. My previously amiable editor suddenly drew back at the mention of spirituality and cautioned me that it wasn't a very popular concept. I agreed with him. However, I pointed out that our need to virtually apologize for using the word "spiritual" in itself signifies a loss of contact with our own spirituality.

Later that evening, when speaking about subtler things that reflect our degree of self-worth, my editor brought up the example of littering, an issue about which he obviously had strong feelings. He suggested that littering is symbolically a negation of the value of others. I agreed with him, but pointed out that the behavior he observed could also be explained as a symptom of spiritual poverty. A litterer's actions reveal a lack of connection with others, and to me, failure to see oneself as an integral part of a whole is primarily a spiritual deficit.

I am not so much concerned here with spirituality as organized religions define it. Rather, I am interested in practical ways of helping people experience and feel connected to this empowering aspect of themselves. I recommend that if you find the terms "spirituality" or "going beyond one's body-mind" objectionable, you can substitute another phrase that makes the basic idea meaningful to you.

Like our genetic inheritance, self-worth is an integral aspect of every person. However, unlike our genetic endowment, which is not affected by our sentiment about it, the quality of our life depends a good deal on how well we develop our self-worth.

We are each as innately capable of experiencing self-worth, as we are of experiencing pain and the drive for pleasure, without having these sensations defined for us. During normal development, we experience these sensations repeatedly before we learn to talk about them. Clearly, such sensations are independent of our ability to define them.

Thinking about our innate capabilities reminds me of the story of the puritanical father, intent on protecting his newborn son from sexual influences. To accomplish this goal, the father raised his son in an environment with no women and without even their mention, and avoided all talk about sexuality. One day, while walking with his father, the boy—then about six years old—happened to see a young girl. With great excitement, the boy turned to his father and asked, "Daddy, what's that?"

Thinking quickly, the father responded, "Oh, that's a—duck!"

"Please, Daddy," begged the boy, his eyes sparkling, "buy me a duck!"

In a similar fashion, I believe that we are each born with a full measure of self-worth, but that measure at first resembles a seed. The seed contains within itself the potential for full growth, but how much of that potential becomes actualized depends on how well it is nurtured. Like a seed sprouting in a forest or garden, the maturing of self-worth is an experiential, not an intellectual process. Indeed, over-intellectualizing about it actually impedes the growth of self-worth.

No definition of love tells us what love really is. Conversely, it is quite possible to know love without studying a single text devoted to its analysis. So too with self-worth. The validity of any definition of self-worth is how well that definition helps us develop a strong, internal sense of self that we actually experience. Inaccurate definitions do not destroy our self-worth, but they can misdirect us in where we seek it, and thus retard its growth. For me, this much is certain: our essence, whatever it is, lies within us. The more we seek our value outside ourselves, the further removed we become from the experience of real self-worth.

If self-worth could be found in things outside ourselves, then people like my patient M.G., whose words begin this chapter, would not be experiencing the lack that she describes. M.G. is youthful, energetic, bright, attractive, fun-loving, happily married with children, creatively employed, financially secure, liked and admired by friends and peers. Yet, she is recurrently depressed and has only a tenuous hold on her feelings of self-worth. She knows that something is missing from her life, and she senses that something is "damaged" or "hidden" within herself. As she works to form and integrate new experiences of mind, body, and spirit, the aching void within her is beginning to disappear. In fact, she is developing self-worth.

## CULTURE AGAINST SELF-WORTH

The self-alienation exhibited by M.G. is far from unique. It is fostered in many ways, both overtly and covertly, by our culture's goal oriented and materialist values. When we examine these values and our culture's messages about individual essence, it becomes clear why poor self-worth has reached epidemic proportions. Just as individuals can, at times, possess a double set of values—those they believe in philosophically and those they actually live by—so can entire cultures. My concern here is not with the philosophical ideals upon which American culture rests, but with their practical translation into the make-a-buck, push-and-shove of everyday life.

In this culture, that which we consider important frequently involves things outside rather than inside ourselves. We rush through our meals gulping down our food, to reach a meeting on time. We let the telephone invade our privacy while we are engaged in important conversations or even while we are making love.

Our work ethic is so strong that most of us define ourselves in terms of our jobs. We often hear people say, "I am an accountant. I am a lawyer. I am a teacher. I am a ----." In doing so, not only do we identify with something external to ourselves, but to make matters worse, we link our identities to jobs which in our society are often ranked in a hierarchy of status. Thus many persons who feel they are stuck in jobs that offer them little day-to-day pride, meaning, or gratification, define themselves in terms of these same jobs.

We have turned to computers to help deal with the complexities of modern society but have yet to confront adequately their dehumanizing side effects. In this regard, some time ago, I traveled a few miles to my local gas and electric company to discuss an incorrect bill. I entered a large lobby in a modern office building and approached the receptionist. After I explained my problem she directed me to one of several comfortable looking chairs ranged about the room and asked me to wait there. When I sat down, I noticed suddenly that each chair had a small table beside it, and that on each table was a telephone.

After sitting for a few minutes, I was startled to hear the ring of the telephone next to my chair. To my surprise, the receptionist signalled me to answer it. I did so, and a pleasant woman's voice inquired how she might help me. I responded that I had come to speak to someone concerning my bill. She assured me that I was speaking to the right person.

"Fine," I replied. "How do I get to your office so that we can discuss the matter?"

Some of the woman's pleasantness faded abruptly, and she said rather tersely, "You cannot come to my office. We can discuss whatever you wish over the phone."

Naively, as I see in retrospect, I replied, "I don't think you understand. I'm already here in the building, down in the lobby."

She interrupted quickly, "Yes, I know that you're in the lobby. But no one comes to our offices. All business is conducted through the phones in the lobby."

Even more naively, I protested, "Look, I could have stayed home and called you. I drove all the way here because I wanted to meet with someone."

She interrupted me again, this time more sharply. "I'm sorry. It's company policy. No one is allowed upstairs."

I persisted, "Well, I'd like to speak with someone in charge. I've never heard of anything like this."

"Then, hang up and someone will call you back."

I waited several minutes until the supervisor called, but I got no further with her. Finally, I returned to the receptionist at the building's entrance. She seemed genuinely surprised at my displeasure and assured me that this procedure was indeed company policy, and that everyone went along with it. I told her that I couldn't believe that she hadn't gotten many complaints about this detached form of human contact. A bit flustered, she repeated what the supervisor had told me—that in order to make room for the computer equipment necessary to get their job done, employee space was devoted almost entirely to computers. There was little enough space upstairs for employees, let alone for customers who wished to discuss their bills or other matters.

This episode is hardly earthshaking. But a growing number of people in our society tell similar stories of run-ins with computer based bureaucracies, of being treated as an account number, and of being victimized by a system so vast that they feel powerless, frustrated, and insignificant.

We have come to worship youth and physical beauty, and as a rule, the people we see on television, particularly in commercials, are quite physically attractive. We watch them hour after hour, as if most of the world were inhabited by such beautiful persons. All this input has led us to accept, perhaps unconsciously, what people, including ourselves, ought to look like. We judge the real people we know by this cultural ideal and as a result become painfully aware of just how much we deviate from it. Similarly, our ideas about how men and women should act are more often influenced by what we see on the screen than by what we see in ourselves. Thus, we tend to distort ourselves physically and emotionally to fit some externally imposed image of what we should be. The result is that we move further away from valuing who we are.

Most of our cities are terrorized daily by crime and violence. Yet, our television programs, movies, and comic books continue to glorify these aspects of life. Certainly, there is an imbalance between the last few moments of the typical program—which perhaps indicate that crime doesn't pay—and the previous thirty to ninety minutes in which brutal crime has been given the spotlight. Cinematic techniques realistically detail each act of violence and make it appear larger than life. Our children regularly watch cartoons that are often more violent and destructive in their content than many films with human characters we might want them to avoid.

It seems clear that such exposure renders us all increasingly insensitive to violent events when they actually occur. We can observe this phenomenon in subtle as well as overt ways. A few weeks ago, a close friend of mine, ordinarily quite caring and compassionate, turned to me with a reassuring expression as we sat in my car stuck in traffic on a rainy night. "It's only an accident," he remarked. "We'll be past it soon."

We reward and define success by the outcome. In sports, the team that wins is not necessarily the one that played the best. We give no rewards to the team that played the best, or got the most pleasure from playing—only to the team that won. Likewise, our business world is structured so that the one who makes it is not necessarily the nicest, fairest, or most honest. We live by the dictum that "money talks" and we generally allow it to talk louder than anything else.

Our educational system too is caught up in success, giving grades that are generally based more on accomplishment than on effort. Academic prowess often relates to how well we have learned to play the game—to memorize and repeat on demand—rather than on how well we can think on our own and learn for ourselves.

For example, I can recall that despite being a very good student, I failed an advanced physics exam in college. Not only did I fail the test, but I didn't answer even one question correctly. What made the situation even more remarkable was that it was an easy examination and that the other students in the class got every answer wrong, too. We later learned that our professor had given the exam as an object lesson.

That is, for some questions he had provided us with more information than was needed to solve the problem. For other questions, he had provided less data than we required to solve the problem, and although we needed only to indicate this, we each struggled even harder to come up with an equation that would yield an answer.

This exam took place in my final year of college—sixteen years into the educational system—yet not one student in this class of bright students could think independently enough to figure out what was happening! We spent a year with that teacher, and none of us passed any of his tests for at least the first half of that time. He kept coming up with new tricks. He was an older man who had only recently returned to teaching after many years of work in industry as a physical chemist. He had decided to go back to classroom teaching because he kept seeing more and more students graduate with the same blunted mind-set as my classmates. His exams reflected his practical experience and required more than book knowledge. Under his tutelage, I learned *to learn*—and in all my years of schooling, only he and one other teacher taught me that. Unfortunately, I don't think my experience in the educational system is unique.

I agree with the nineteenth-century French biophysicist Pierre Lecomte duNouy, who wrote in *Human Destiny:*

> The religious spirit is in us. It preceded the religions, and their task—as well as that of the prophets, or the initiated—consists in releasing, directing, and developing it. The mystical aspiration is an essentially human trait. It slumbers at the bottom of our souls awaiting the event, or the man capable, in the manner of an enzyme, of transforming it into true mysticism, into faith.

In many ways, science has become the most popular religion in our culture. It has its own hierarchy of priests (academic levels), temples (laboratories), and cathedrals (universities). It has its own language, its own inviolate commandments and rituals, and its own unproven axioms and dogma. Science insists that it is the ultimate measure of truth and validity. Most people accept science so completely that they don't even recognize that it is actually a religion or belief system. For them, scientific fact is the highest level of proof attainable in the universe.

Albert Einstein, perhaps the most revered scientist of the age, in his own way challenged religious belief in science. His theory of relativity called into question the claim of scientists that they possessed some unalterable, ultimate truth. Despite Einstein's valiant efforts and countless examples of scientific fallability, many today continue to believe that the scientific worldview is the only valid or credible one. To adopt a rigidly held scientific worldview is to reject aspects of ourselves that do not function by logic. By devaluing and disconnecting from parts of our humanness, we dampen our sense of self-worth.

Thus, science and technology have failed us. Or, if you prefer, we have failed them. While science can undoubtedly make life easier by day-to-day standards, it cannot give us a sense of meaning or self-worth.

We have looked to psychiatry too for ultimate answers and the means to create a better society. Many practitioners and their intellectual allies believed that applying psychoanalytic principles to individuals would eventually change society as a whole, but this dream has proven illusory. For one thing, though psychiatry is rooted in the medical model, it immediately goes awry when it establishes a sharp, uneven distinction between doctor and patient. Too, mainstream medicine is symptom rather than person oriented. As a physician, I know all too well that medical training is reductionistic and that our preferred approach to healing is to prescribe pills. Wellness is defined as an absence of overt signs of illness, not as the sense of well-being and optimal health that should be the goal for all of us. Nor is preventive medicine commonly practiced. Few doctors bother to obtain a detailed history of their patients' diet and nutritional supplements, degree and type of physical exercise, daily job or family stresses, normal patterns of breathing and relaxation, or habitual exposure to sunlight and fresh air. Certainly, most physicians spend the bulk of their working time treating illnesses rather than preventing them. Perhaps psychiatry is more health oriented than most medical specialties. But it too has adopted the values dominant in our society and emphasizes the most superficial aspects of our being.

## CARRYING THE DONKEY

Our culture directs us away from our inner centers and sources of self-worth in many subtle ways. The widespread use of ballpoint pens is a trivial but revealing example. On several occasions, I have watched a master of Chinese calligraphy practice his art. I listened to him explain how each brush stroke does more than make a line on paper; it expresses the energy and emotion of the word being written. At first, I found calligraphy simply interesting or entertaining. I certainly saw no practical use for writing in this way. "What difference does it make?" I thought. "As long as the reader understands the writing, who cares whether the words are written with carefully executed brush strokes or hurriedly with a ballpoint pen?"

It took me a while to find an answer, because I failed to realize how goal oriented my question was.

As I watched the calligraphy master over a period of weeks, I remembered how differently I had viewed writing during my early years of school. Because we used a straight pen and ink, we had to be attentive to the technical parts of writing—caring for the ink, pen, and paper, redipping the point after a few strokes, slowly forming the words, and using a blotter or patiently waiting for the ink to dry. The act of writing required more concentration, more neatness, and more time than it does now with ballpoint pens. I think we've lost something real yet intangible as a result.

If while writing, we are concerned only with communicating a message to another person, then it truly makes no difference whether our words are typed, handwritten, or even scratched on wood with a nail, so long as the goal of communication is fulfilled. However, as we shall see in Chapter 3, *to focus solely on the goal is to remove ourselves from the beauty of the process.* If we are involved in writing, then writing ought to be more than merely a means of communicating. It should be a way to express ourselves and allow us to relate more fully to the task at hand.

In the past, writing was also a more sensuous experience—the delicate odor of the ink, the gentle sound of the point scratching on the paper, the visual delight of the ink flowing and changing color as it dried. All of these aspects enabled us to be involved more personally with writing than we are when simply sending a message.

In short, as the mechanics of writing became easier, our involvement in the process diminished. The fountain pen let us write faster and do away with the inkwell. The ballpoint pen produced a far more dramatic change—writing could be done smoothly, instantly, and with a minimum of concentration. Caring for the writing utensil became unnecessary. Soon, the ballpoint pen was so inexpensive that it was disposable. When was the last time you bought a refill for a ballpoint pen? Are pen refills even manufactured anymore?

Just as I grew up in an era when quills were no longer used as writing instruments, the younger generation today has known nothing but ballpoint pens. Now, I am not advocating that we turn back the technological clock and write with older methods. Nor do I believe that we should return to the horse and buggy and end automobile production. Rather, I am pointing out that with each technological improvement, we lose something in spite of the time we supposedly save. Living in such a goal oriented culture shapes us in countless small ways every day.

We are not only alienated from tasks outside of ourselves, like writing. Many of us are also in poor contact with our own bodies, and thus have never learned the basics of how to care for ourselves physically. We tend to live in our heads, although we generally exert only minimal control over our thoughts. Typically, we are resigned to being victims of internal and external circumstances in life. When we do turn inward, we characteristically examine our intellects, not our feelings. We downplay imagination ("it's only your imagination"), intuition ("don't be silly"), and emotions ("be brave; don't let on how you feel"). In doing so, we cut ourselves off from essential parts of ourselves.

By overemphasizing intellectual activity, we end up revering authority figures at the expense of our own opinions. As a physician, I see this phenomenon all the time with my patients. For example, a young woman to whom I had recommended the poetic novel *Jonathan Livingston Seagull* repeatedly asked me, "Did Jonathan die at the end of the story?" Although she had obviously read the novel as competently as I had, she somehow could not trust her own interpretation. As a psychiatrist, I represented unquestionable authority to her. No doubt, she would even have abandoned her own interpretation of the story had I offered her a different version.

It is common practice for us to judge ourselves by how we think others see us. Thus, instead of relying on our internal sensations for direction, we are encouraged to feel happy when others seem to like us and to feel sad when they apparently do not. This process leads to a self-negating kind of people pleasing.

There is an old story illustrating this phenomenon, about a grandfather, his grandson, and a donkey. One summer day, the three were ambling toward town when they passed a stranger. He stopped them to point out how silly it was for the old man and the boy to be walking when they had a perfectly adequate donkey to carry them. Hearing the stranger's words, the pair climbed onto the donkey and continued their journey.

Soon they passed another stranger, who scowled at them, "Have you no mercy? The poor beast must be aching under your weight! Don't you think that the two of you riding on that small creature's back is painful to it?"

The grandson immediately got off and led the donkey, which was now carrying only the grandfather. Soon, they encountered another passerby, who spoke angrily to the old man, "You're perfectly capable of walking! Why do you tire out the donkey and the boy? You should walk and let the child sit instead!"

Hearing this, the grandfather changed places with

his grandson. It was not long, however, before they were accosted by yet another stranger, who found new fault with them. "You should be ashamed of yourself!" he said to the child. "Riding on the donkey when your grandfather, who is so much older, must walk on this hot day! Have you no respect for your elders?"

The boy got off the donkey. He looked at his grandfather, and his grandfather looked back at him. There seemed only one thing left to do. They hoisted the donkey onto their backs and carried it as they trudged into town.

As absurd as this story may seem, we all often act like the boy and his grandfather. In a useless effort to please everybody, we too end up carrying the donkey.

Consistent with such a self-defeating outlook, we try to fit our desires to the expectations of others. For instance, one of my patients recently felt depressed because several weeks earlier she had agreed to attend a party, and now she no longer felt like going. "I wish I still wanted to go to the party," she said sadly. Actually, she did not enjoy parties much at all, but she wanted to be the kind of person who does. She saw herself as sick emotionally because what she wanted did not fit the image of what she had decided she was *supposed* to want!

It is easy to provide countless examples of this situation in our lives. But my intention is not sociological analysis. I have purposely chosen anecdotes to which most of us can relate to make one simple point: Our culture is inundating us with the message that our worth lies in money, power, external success, and mass popularity—all things that lie outside ourselves. This message is very strong and pervasive. It touches us all and hooks all who are unwary. The more we accept this message as personally valid and structure our lives around it, the further we move from our inner center.

And the more we lose contact with a sense of life's meaning and our own self-worth.

## GETTING CENTERED

I don't, however, wish to attack our culture *ad nauseum*. Such a stance is neither very useful nor wholly sensible. For instance, in her provocative book *Centering*, M. C. Richards writes:

> Our muddle about spirit in man and universe has been in the making for a few centuries only. It may be the price we have paid for our mastery, such as it is, over the physical world. In the history of consciousness, it seems as if man had to store away for awhile his sense of worth and meaning in order to cultivate [scientific] aptitudes. . . . In order to develop certain mechanical abilities, he has had perhaps to neglect his spiritual institutions. . . . [But] this age has its positive contribution to make to man's evolution: an image of life in which man can center his machine, his work, and his values. (pp. 49-50)

To establish a better balance, we can change our present culture, ourselves, or perhaps both. Sometimes, we project our shortcomings onto our surroundings and then get stuck because we expect solutions to arise only when our environment changes. For example, one of my patients described herself as a harassed schoolteacher and complained constantly about the "lousy" urban school system that employed her. Despite the school system's real inadequacies, I began to see that my patient's real problem was her outlook. To stave off feelings of insecurity, she felt compelled to make people like her. Outside of school, her circle of acquaintances was small and select, and she was generally able to find ways of pleasing them. But within the complex network of coworker relationships at school, she could not please everybody. She misinterpreted the anxiety that she thereby experienced as evidence of the school system's inadequacies, rather than her own.

Sometimes, the path to increased self-worth leads us into beneficial, unforeseen territory. We change in ways that we could not possibly have consciously planned. But perhaps some deeper part of ourselves knows where the Self is headed. When I was a little boy, I loved ice cream malteds. Occasionally, my brother and I were able to go to a neighborhood luncheonette where to our utter delight we would order a malted. I kept thinking that when I was grown up and had money of my own, I would come back to one of these luncheonettes, order a dozen ice cream malteds, and drink them one after the other.

This image was very vivid, and for years I harbored this fantasy. I knew that once I could afford the dozen ice cream malteds, I would certainly make the dream come true. But somewhere in the process of maturation, things changed. I have long since been able to afford the dozen malteds, but have I ever fulfilled my fantasy? Of course not. Nor have I ever been tempted to do so. The same thing happened to my childhood love of playing cowboys and Indians. As a boy, I could never understand my parents' disdain for joining me in that wonderful game. I was sure that when I became a father, I would spend my leisure time playing cowboys and Indians. But that fantasy too disappeared with my childhood toys. Somewhere in the process of growing, things change.

Inner growth is not always what we expect. Nor is it always without painful moments. When facing such moments, we may find the following analogy helpful. I heard it from a psychiatrist, Dr. Alexander Lowen, founder of bioenergetic analysis. It is about a man whose hand becomes frostbitten when he is caught in a subzero winter storm. At first, the bitter cold caused the man's hand to hurt, but as he continued to expose his hand to the icy temperature, it gradually became numb. Eventually, there was no more pain.

With a frozen but pain-free hand, the man came upon an empty cottage in the forest. He entered and found a roaring fire in the fireplace. The heat felt good against his body, but as he extended his frostbitten hand towards the flame, he experienced excruciating pain and quickly yanked his hand away. Thawing out a frostbitten limb can be very painful. The man now had a choice. He could keep his hand away from the heat and avoid the pain. Or, he could undergo the pain and be able to use his hand again. In one form or another, this is the choice that we must all make in our lives.

There is much good in Western culture, and there are even positive aspects to the examples I have presented in this chapter. Our task is not to abandon our culture in favor of some supposed Eastern utopia. If we look to any of the contemporary Asian societies, we certainly find turmoil and unrest. There is no evidence that most Asian people have achieved inner tranquillity and contentment. Rather, for those of us who choose to live within Western culture, my goal is to provide practical ways for counteracting its destructive effects on our self-worth.

Like people in all cultures and times, our task in life is to strike a balance, so that we not only benefit from our surroundings, but contribute to them in a way that promotes true growth for everyone.

# 2

# Pouring Water: Growing Self-Worth

*The task of man is to become what he is.*
Karlfried Durckheim

There are practical methods that each of us can use to enhance our sense of self-worth. Superficially, some of these techniques may seem nonsensical or unrelated to our feelings of individual worthiness. But an exclusively intellectual approach to these methods cannot lead to a full understanding of their purpose, just as an exclusively intellectual exploration of music falls short of a total appreciation of music. Rather, the process of growing personal self-worth, like getting in touch with music, is essentially experiential.

To understand this notion, imagine a man who knows nothing about how a tree grows. He knows what a tree *is*, because he sees trees every day. But he has never learned anything about botany and hasn't the faintest inkling of what is involved in the maturation of a tree. Now, suppose that after having made the necessary soil preparation, you have just planted a seed to grow a tree. You have covered the seed with earth, and you are in the midst of pouring water from a bucket onto the ground where the seed has been planted, when the man happens to come by. He sees what you are doing, but thinks little of it. The next day, however, his curiosity is aroused when he sees you emerge from your house with a full bucket, carry it to the same spot of land, and pour the water again. As time goes by, the man sees you perform this strange, apparently ritualistic action every day. One day, when you are not around, he steps over to the watered spot and inspects it carefully. The spot certainly appears no different from any of the surrounding land. The man now begins to wonder whether perhaps something is mentally wrong with you.

Wanting to give you the benefit of the doubt, he stops you one day as you stand over the spot, bucket in hand. "What are you doing?" he queries.

"Oh," you answer casually, "I'm growing a tree."

Now, he *knows* that you're daft. After all, he is familiar with trees. He has seen thousands of them, and he can see plainly that you have produced as much of a tree as Hans Christian Andersen's emperor was wearing new clothes.

Having seen enough, the man might well choose to leave at this point. He might enjoy some good laughs talking about you to his friends. However, if he decides instead to wait around to see how long you will keep up this foolishness—and if he waits around long enough—one day the man will see something emerging from the ground, at that precise place where for many weeks or months you have been pouring the water.

At last, the man might realize that perhaps you have been growing a tree. As he watches the sapling get bigger, he might even decide to grow a tree of his own. So imagine now that the man obtains an identical bucket, fills it with water, selects a place where he would like to see a tree, and pours the water on that spot. Faithfully mimicking your actions, he pours a bucket of water over his special spot each day. He fully expects that he, like you, will some day grow a tree!

When it comes to self-worth, most of us resemble the man who knew what trees are, but not how they grow. Generally, we recognize self-worth when we see it. At times, we feel a measure of it within ourselves, and often we can tell when we are with someone who possesses it. Yet, like the man, few of us know much or even anything about how to grow self-worth for ourselves.

## WATER-POURING EXERCISES

It is valuable to remember the analogy of the man and the tree as we start to explore the variety of techniques and exercises that have been available for centuries for nurturing self-worth. At first, many of these methods may make no more sense to us than did the act of pouring water on the ground to the man who knew nothing about tree growing. At the outset it is rarely possible to see any connection between particular, seemingly ritualistic daily techniques and our goal of enhancing self-worth. Thus, I have chosen to call these tasks "water-pouring exercises."

When we insist that understanding must precede experiencing, we elevate the rational part of our mind above other parts of ourselves: we assume that logic is the ultimate test of validity. This attitude is not only arrogant, but also self-defeating emotionally, physically, and spiritually. It is arrogant because it suggests that logic is our most accurate way to gain knowledge, and consequently, that ideas that do not fit the logical system be discarded as false. It is also self-defeating because our sense of self-worth does not derive from nor is it a measure of our capacity for logic. To idolize logic in this way moves us more into our ego and further from our inner center, thus diminishing our awareness of self.

Think how ludicrous it must have sounded before the discovery of the microscope and its confirmation of the existence of bacteria to hear someone declare, "I can tell you what causes disease. You are sick because tiny, invisible living things that float through the air have gotten into your body. Once these invisible things get inside you, they start to reproduce until there are millions and millions of them. Even then you can't see them, but they are powerful enough to weaken or even kill you."

During certain periods of history, a person could have been burned at the stake for espousing such heresy or seeming witchcraft. However, once the microscope was invented and microbes could be clearly seen, then this heresy was deemed inviolate scientific truth, and we all became fervent believers. The way the discovery of microbes changed people's thinking about disease is characteristic of how humans have related to science through history. In light of this tendency, ask yourself whether you believe that all the scientific instruments with which we can gain a better understanding of the universe have already been invented. Surely they have not, and yet to acknowledge this fact is to admit that things exist in the cosmos beyond our current understanding.

We need not devalue our present knowledge, but we also need not limit ourselves to what science is capable of comprehending at this moment. This observation is especially true in areas where human experience has gone beyond its current rational understanding. In some situations, seeking to grasp an event intellectually at an inappropriate time can hinder or even block the event from occurring.

For instance, much is known about the physiology of sexual orgasm. However, if we try to analyze its precise mechanics during lovemaking our pleasurable experience of orgasm would likely be greatly diminished or altogether inhibited. In such situations, as in some of the water-pouring exercises in this book, we should not abandon our intellectual faculty. But at times, we should set rational analysis aside so that we can more fully experience ourselves. In other words, a more complete understanding can emerge *from the experience itself.*

I believe that only after we have developed a strong sense of self-worth can we begin to comprehend the subtleties of its underlying growth process. Only then can we look back on the particular technique we employed and say, "Yes, now I see why it was necessary, how it helped me to grow."

Admittedly, the fact that knowledge comes only retrospectively makes our task more difficult initially because we must start our inner journey without full understanding. It is precisely this difficulty that dissuades many people from beginning and that discourages many beginners from advancing in their efforts. But to return to our analogy, we have to wait around long enough to see something sprouting from the ground.

It is easy in our state of ignorance to dismiss potent methods of inner growth as worthless or even crazy. At the other extreme, it is easy in our state of eagerness and blind faith to embrace methods of growth that are actually worthless and crazy. However, not only the cynical and the gullible can become deceived or disheartened. All of us in between may err on one side or the other when we are confronted with a path that promises to enhance our self-worth.

My best advice in this context is that you stick to the study and practice of water-pouring exercises that have successfully transcended time and culture. In this book, therefore, I have focused on methods that have been performed for centuries, by people in a variety of cultures around the globe. Why? Because I believe that truths about human nature have found expression in many historical periods and cultures. Those truths that seem to have been rediscovered in every generation and in many cultures will therefore be the basis of the program I present.

However, I must add a word of caution: No matter how valid a particular exercise might be for increasing our self-worth, learning how to perform it and even performing it regularly, does not automatically guarantee success. Take meditation as an example. It is possible to learn a meditative technique, set aside time each day to practice it, and conscientiously perform the technique as prescribed. Yet if these actions are merely mechanical, even such a powerful technique as meditation will have no effect. No matter how real it may look, a mechanical form of meditation—even if practiced for years—will do little or nothing to enhance our feeling of self-worth. For such a method to be effective, it must be undertaken with appropriate expectations and with a special type of discipline. Neither of these prerequisites can be mastered mechanically or routinely.

Moreover, you must first carry out adequate preparations. We left our tree man pouring water onto the ground and expecting a tree to grow. We know that no tree will emerge because he failed to precede his watering with the necessary preparation. Out of ignorance, the man not only neglected to plant a seed, but he also neglected to prepare the ground. Before planting, it is usually necessary to weed the ground, till the soil, and fertilize the earth. Without such preparation, no amount of well-meaning expectation or conscientious, disciplined watering is likely to yield a tree.

## PATIENCE: THE HIDDEN KEY

But let us not be too hard on the man. It is not uncommon to want to skip the preparations and proceed immediately to the real thing. This is especially true when the preparations seem difficult, boring, or not particularly relevant to our goal. Nevertheless, this human tendency to underestimate the value of preparation can actually prevent us from attaining our objective.

For example, imagine that although you have never studied physics, you have become extremely interested in quantum mechanics. You are pleased to discover that this advanced topic is being taught right now at your local university, and you quietly enter the classroom to hear the appropriate lecture. The professor has just begun speaking, and is already filling up the first blackboard with Greek symbols and mathematical equations.

Now, because you have never studied high school or college physics, it is unlikely that you will learn very much from the professor's talk. It is not that the information is being hidden. On the contrary, the facts of quantum mechanics are being presented openly and straightforwardly to the class. Nor is it that you are being deliberately excluded from absorbing the subject matter. Rather, you are unable to understand what the professor is teaching because you lack the necessary background information. It is no doubt true that mastering all the mathematical formulas of high school and college physics would not answer your questions about quantum mechanics. But those courses would have prepared you to understand the answers when you finally encountered them.

Similarly, the methods to increase self-worth are readily available. But we must first prepare ourselves to benefit from these methods. Thus, the water-pouring exercises to follow are actually ways of heightening our overall consciousness. The development of self-worth is actually a by-product of that process. To understand this distinction can sometimes help to keep our frustration level down, because it means that we do not need to wait until we have reached the highest states of consciousness before we strengthen our self-worth.

In a typical school situation, we need to graduate to get a diploma. If the school offers a four-year program, and we complete only three-and-a-half years, no matter how well we have been doing academically, we will not get a diploma. But in the program of personal growth for which water-pouring exercises are required, we do not need to wait until graduation to be rewarded with enhanced self-worth. The process itself may be challenging or arduous, but whatever gains we make are ours from the first moment onwards.

In short, our *self-worth is increased by participating in the process and not as a result of completing it.*

The following chapters describe a variety of methods for improving self-worth, each constituting a different path to the same place. These techniques are not mutually exclusive, and it is possible to integrate the practice of several or even all of them. Yet, it is also possible to increase self-worth through the practice of only a single technique.

In conclusion, I would like to return once again to the tree-man who represents each of us searching for self-worth. None of us can make a tree. But given a seed, we can do much to nurture its growth.

So too with self-worth. We cannot create self-worth where it doesn't exist. But I believe that self-worth is inherent in the human life process: it is an inborn and inseparable part of every person. Like a seed, it must be properly cared for in order to grow. When its development is inhibited, as it is by many of our culture's influences, self-worth is not destroyed, but rather becomes dormant. With appropriate care, its growth process can be renewed. There is no age limit to this miracle. It can begin for each of us whenever we are ready.

# 3

# Going to the Circus: Balancing Goals and Process

*Suddenly, I remembered that I had forgotten to remember myself.*

P. D. Ouspensky

The best way I know to demonstrate that people in Western society tend to be too goal oriented is to share a personal experience. Many years ago, when my wife and I had first come to live in Rockland County outside New York City, we heard that the circus was coming to town. We told our three young children that we would take them to the circus, a prospect that created great anticipation. All week long, the children talked about nothing except what the circus would be like. In a moment of extreme generosity or foolishness, I had agreed to take along my friend's two children as well. When the fateful morning arrived, the five children and I piled into the station wagon.

As I drove out of my quiet, tree lined neighborhood toward the Palisades Parkway, one of the children suddenly asked, "Are we there yet?"

Smiling broadly, I answered, "Nope, we've just started. We have a long way to go."

A few minutes passed. Then another child asked, "Are we there yet?"

Still smiling, I replied, "No, we're not there."

Several more times one of the children would ask me the same question. Gradually, I stopped smiling and felt myself becoming irritated. I could feel the edge in my voice as I heard myself saying, "No, we're not there yet! I've already told you!"

Eventually, their questioning grew more shrill. Finally, I heard myself shouting, "That does it! If one more person back there asks me, 'Are we there yet?' I'm going to stop the car, turn it around, and take all of us home! And I mean it! I've had it with you kids!"

That scene is familiar enough to anyone who has raised children, or even been around them. But then something strange occurred. At the very moment that I was shouting angrily about turning back, I suddenly understood what was happening in the car. It was my first clear insight into the issue of process and goal. That is, I understood that the five children were so goal oriented, so bent on getting to the circus, that the process, the journey, had almost no meaning whatsoever. They were wishing the entire trip away so that they could be at their destination immediately. It also occurred to me that since these were my children, they must have acquired this intense goal orientation from me.

My angry threat was apparently taken seriously by those in the backseat, for silence now reigned in the car. For the remainder of the drive into Manhattan, I wondered: Was I really seeing myself in my children's impatience and restlessness? The more I pondered the matter, the more the answer seemed an inescapable yes.

At last the six of us arrived at the circus. To my utter amazement, within half an hour the children began whining, "What are we going to do *next* week?" I was dismayed and flabbergasted. They had finally reached the circus, which they had excitedly anticipated for days. Now that they were finally there, they were spending their time worrying about how to occupy themselves next week instead of enjoying the event at hand.

I understood that once the children had achieved their goal of getting to the circus, they needed a new goal, something even more exciting to anticipate for tomorrow or for next week. I realized at that moment that the circus could symbolize anything special that we anticipate. As adults, we have our own circuses for which we plan intensely—an upcoming party, a vacation, or an expensive new house, car, or other purchase.

During the show's intermission, as my children grew increasingly restless and bored, I asked myself: Looking back at my own life, how many circuses have I actually experienced? How much time do I spend at the circus as compared to the time I spend anticipating and preparing to attend? The answers became unmistakably clear. I really experience very few circuses, but I spend a lot of time going to them.

As I reflected further that afternoon at Madison Square Garden, I realized that the children could have done many things during that hour riding from our home in Rockland County. They could have had fun in the car, looking at their surroundings, talking and joking amongst themselves. But because they had been so fixated on their destination, they experienced only restlessness and dissatisfaction.

But in all fairness to the children, I must ask what kind of example had I set? I had been at the wheel of that station wagon, feeling little but anticipatory tension too. None of us in the car had understood that we were wasting our lives waiting to reach the symbolic circus. As the final act of clowns and animals bombastically ended, I realized that my daily attitude would have to change. Otherwise, I would experience only a few precious moments of delight and a lifetime of moments wished away or ignored.

Now, I am not suggesting that there is anything wrong with establishing goals for ourselves. Rather, my point is that we need balance. In our culture, we have lost the harmony between seeking goals and enjoying process. We are too involved with objectives and too little involved with what we experience while striving for them.

People who are too goal oriented eventually become depressed. Studies of suicide attempts show that suicides often occur during times when individuals are externally successful, in fact, when they have achieved a goal. A person might fantasize, "I'll reach this goal, obtain my diploma, have a baby, become vice president of the company—and then I'll feel good about myself." Believing this, the person remains busy and focused. However, too often when the goal is realized, the person becomes profoundly depressed.

Many patients come to me for help because they feel desperately unhappy though they are outwardly quite successful. For example, Louis is a forty-two-year-old businessman in a key position at a major international corporation based in New York City. Materially, he lacks nothing. His marriage is good; he is respected by his peers and admired by the many employees he manages. Yet, he is extremely depressed, though few know it.

Louis lives almost entirely inside his head. His body feels almost nothing. With each outward success, his inner deadness spreads. It is not so much that Louis cannot establish goals, though finding new goals is increasingly difficult. Rather, he has finally come to see his illusions as illusions. He has achieved in adulthood all that he aimed for, but he nevertheless has none of what he hoped to obtain. Thus his emptiness remains. Louis's previous attempts at psychotherapy have not really helped, and he desperately wants to know if there is another way.

Where do I begin? I tell him about my experience going to the circus. He is initially skeptical, then intrigued. Gradually, Louis begins to experience the simple joys of daily life. His emptiness begins to recede.

So it is for each of us. We can all learn to get more in touch with the process of life, rather than being trapped by the goals we set for ourselves. *The more we can enjoy the trip to the circus, the less important it becomes whether we ever get there.*

This is not to suggest that goals are bad or unnecessary. Of course, being overly passive is un unhealthy mental condition as well. Sitting around lethargically without meaningful goals in life is not desirable either.

Certainly, goals are important in negotiating the material world, the world of the many. Without goals, we lack direction and motivation. Our lives contain no logic and no passion.

In fact, having goals is inherent in the concept of life force. As psychiatrist Wilhelm Reich emphasized, all biological organisms build up energy that seeks discharge. This discharge can be either directed or random. Goals create direction for the discharge of personal energy and thereby provide meaningful structure to our lives. To abandon all goals is to abandon order.

Because we humans have an inherent need to avoid chaos and its resulting anxiety, we must have goals. The issue is not to eliminate goals but rather to reevaluate their overriding importance. Much of the time, we allow the goals we establish to overshadow our lives, instead of letting our goals serve as avenues along which we can enjoy our lives more fully.

## SEXUALITY AND LETTING GO OF GOALS

In the area of sexuality, we too often stifle daily joy by our overconcern with objectives. Lovemaking is a process, whereas sexual orgasm is a goal. We lose so much pleasure and generate so much frustration and anger when the goal of orgasm eclipses the process of getting there. As a psychiatrist, I hear countless complaints from my patients about their sexuality, concerns over whether they're experiencing orgasm, how frequently they experience it, and how long it typically takes to achieve it. I hear very little about the process of lovemaking, but a great deal about its supposed goal or objective.

Of course, this situation is hardly surprising. How we act sexually is a reflection of our everyday behavior in the world, for our way of being expresses itself in all aspects of life. Goal oriented living begets goal oriented sexuality, and consequently our widespread sexual dysfunctions and dissatisfactions.

Now I am not suggesting that we abandon sexual orgasm or our desire for it. Rather, I propose that we recognize that the more we emphasize orgasm—our own, and even more disasterously, our partner's—the less involved we are in the moment-to-moment delights of lovemaking. Most of our sexual problems can be resolved if we simply maintain meaningful contact during the act of love. For many of us, this involves an overall change in our values and way of being in the world. When we shift from anticipating the circus to enjoying the trip, many sexual difficulties disappear.

The case of my colleague Vincent offers a vivid example. Vincent is a tall, good-looking, soft-spoken, sensitive, middle-aged man who works as a psychiatrist. We have been friends for many years. He is more comfortable taking in his environment than actively impressing himself upon it. He seems depressed much of the time, and occasionally says that he is dissatisfied with his life. Once we attended a growth workshop together in which Vincent spoke openly about his unhappiness, which emanated, he felt, from his sexual inadequacy.

Vincent explained that although his wife was satisfied with him as a sexual partner, and he with her, he nevertheless felt dismayed about his lack of prowess. He had a clear image of how he should be in bed—strong, aggressive, and even overpowering. He wanted his lovemaking to be controlled, hard, and vigorous. But Vincent knew that he was none of these things, either in bed or out of it. He was a quiet, caring man: a gentle soul who wanted to be an aggressive lover.

Our workshop leader, Stanley Keleman, a gifted psychotherapist and teacher, understood Vincent's dilemma. With great skill, he was able to guide Vincent to see that there are many ways to be a real man, many ways to be strong. Keleman led Vincent to see that his strength lay in his softness and gentleness, and that when he tried to achieve a false image of manhood, he ultimately betrayed himself.

Vincent's depression, therefore, resulted from not only his frustrating pursuit of a sexual goal, but also from his having selected a goal that denied his true nature.

## ATHLETIC ENJOYMENTS VERSUS GOALS

Our professional and even amateur sports and games are also structured to reflect the importance we attach to goals. Winning is everything; certainly it is more significant than the physical pleasure and emotional enjoyment of recreation. Because of our emphasis on winning, we sophisticated adults typically experience much less satisfaction during our leisure hours than do children.

My patient Louis, who works as a lawyer, talks to me about tennis. Louis loves to play tennis. He rates himself an intermediate player, who enjoys tennis for its vigorous exercise, and for its demands on skill, coordination, speed, and quick thinking. Louis wants to play for the sheer joy of the sport, yet inevitably, as soon as a game gets underway, he becomes tense about winning.

Louis is no fool. He begins each match with the desire to stay relaxed, to be involved in moment-to-moment play, rather than in the outcome. He wants to experience physical satisfaction as he runs and swings his racket. Sometimes, he feels this satisfaction for a short while before he tenses up. But once the goal of winning becomes dominant, Louis loses his smoothly flowing strokes and hits choppy shots in an attempt to win the point quickly. When this happens, Louis no longer enjoys the game physically.

Like Louis, most adults become tense and driven whenever they participate in sports. The problem is not in our desire to win the game. There is nothing intrinsically wrong with that outlook. Rather, the difficulty comes when we start feeling good or bad about ourselves for having won or lost—when the pleasure inherent in each moment of play is replaced by worrying about the score. Often we define ourselves athletically in terms of what opponents we beat or what opponents beat us. When winning becomes an overriding goal, we lose an opportunity to experience the aliveness of our bodies in motion, and with it, an opportunity to strengthen our self-worth.

Similarly, because winning is more important to Louis than playing, he allows poker games to strain his friendships, bridge matches to stress his marriage, and board games like Monopoly to cause family fights. Louis does want to change. He knows that in describing his style of tennis, he is describing his entire approach to life. Louis also knows that if he can effect the change he seeks on the tennis court, then he will approach the rest of his life differently. Ultimately, he will change his entire way of being.

So, we work together to help Louis become a different kind of tennis player. I do not teach him different strokes or help him with his court strategy. Instead, I teach him deep breathing, centering, and many of the other techniques discussed in this book. We both know that Louis's sense of self-worth does not depend on how Louis deals with his court opponents. Rather, the key is Louis's ability to win an inner game of tennis between himself and his own desire for mastery.

## THE NEED TO BE IN CONTROL

The physical control we seek in sports has a parallel in the emotional control we seek in other areas of our life. Consciously and unconsciously, we typically seek to maintain emotional control in every situation. As a result, we frequently lose the pleasure of spontaneity in everyday life. Sometimes, emotional control can be beneficial; it helps us become better organized and more efficient, dependable, and industrious. However, always striving to achieve the goal of control interferes with the process of getting in touch with our feelings.

Too often we subordinate our feelings to logic, which we erroneously view as a necessary step to attaining self-control. When we experience strong emotions that seem incomprehensible, many of us believe we are losing control or coping poorly. Yet, feelings are not at all dependent on logic. When we observe very young children, we see a wide range of emotions: love, anger, happiness, sadness, fear, and jealousy. Such emotions are present for years before adult logic as we know it becomes part of the human organism.

Logic must be developed. If in our parental impatience we ask our children, "Why are you crying?" we imply that there must be a reason, and that the reason must be understood and verbalized. When we declare, "That's no reason to cry!" or say "If you don't stop that silly crying, I'll give you a real reason to cry!" we further imply that the child's reasons for crying must conform to adult logic. This tendency illustrates how we've been taught, and then perpetuate, the myth that human feelings must make sense. When they do not, we often deny their right to exist.

In the emotional system that most of us have internalized, being in control is synonymous with being reasonable or sensible. We forget that our feelings are not dependent on logic, and consequently we employ logic to judge our feelings. This process always becomes self-denigrating and ends up dampening our spontaneity. How often do we tell ourselves: "I know I'm silly for feeling this," or "I feel so stupid because I know there's nothing to be sad about," or "I become so embarrassed whenever I feel this."

When we become ashamed or intolerant of certain emotions, we carefully shield them from other people. The less logical our feeling, the more unacceptable it seems to our self-image, and the greater our repression. Ultimately, to stay in control, we make the devastating sacrifice of hiding our feelings from ourselves. In this way, we become estranged from our needs and rhythms and separated from our sense of self. Sadly, we surrender basic sources of self-worth to external judgments, expectations, and responses.

## EMOTIONS: CENTERED IN THE BODY

In my therapeutic work, I have found that when most of us talk about our feelings, we refer almost exclusively to a mental awareness, rather than to a body experience. Numbing our bodies is another means through which we stay in control and distance ourselves from our feelings. Quite literally, in order for us to feel something, we must move some part of our bodies. By restricting body motion, we limit the intensity of our feelings. For instance, when a limb is immobilized, we gradually lose sensation in it. To regain feeling, we must move the arm or the leg.

The word "emotion" comes from the root *exmovere*, which means "to move away." Thus even our language recognizes the connection between body and feeling: We "jump for joy;" we are "moved to tears;" and we become so excited that we "can't sit still."

Every emotion is associated with a particular physical sensation. In fact, it is our experience of this body sensation that makes us cognitively aware of the emotion. We need only pay attention to our own bodies. Often, my patients are surprised when I ask, "Where do you feel what you're describing right now?" The question puzzles those who conceptualize feelings as something they experience in their heads, much as they do their more abstract thoughts. Often, my question focuses their attention on their bodies and enables them to become aware that they do experience distinct physical sensations along with their emotions.

On an unconscious level, we always recognize our feelings. This is hardly surprising, for keeping our emotions unconscious is a powerful way of controlling their intensity. The more we live in our heads rather than in our total being, the more we cherish control and seek methods of preventing our feelings from getting too strong.

Labeling the physical sensations that emotions trigger when they do become conscious is one way we keep feelings tightly under control. For example, sadness generally manifests as a physical sensation—often as a heaviness in the chest. We can either stay with that sensation and experience it deeply, or give it a label and say, "I am sad." Then, we can talk about being sad rather than experiencing the sadness in our total being.

Mislabeling our feelings is an even more potent means of control. When we mislabel a feeling we can deal with a substitute emotion rather than the emotion we are really experiencing. My patient Barbara provided a vivid example of this tendency. An attractive, twenty-two-year-old woman, Barbara was participating in a therapeutic group I was leading when she suddenly declared, "I feel very depressed." Barbara told the group that she had experienced such episodes, each lasting a few days, during the past three years. This particular period of depression had begun the night before the session and had continued since then.

When I asked where she was feeling depressed, Barbara initially seemed not to understand my question. I asked her to focus on her body and to describe what she was feeling. Soon she pointed to her abdomen and said, "I feel a sense of pressure right here." Barbara explained that the pressure felt unpleasant, almost painful, and remembered that this pressure always accompanied her depressions.

I encouraged Barbara to stay with her feeling of pressure and, despite its unpleasantness, experience it as fully as possible without resistance. For the next several moments, Barbara did not attempt to suppress the pressure nor seek to label it. Soon she reported that her abdominal pain was diminishing. Within moments she experienced a strong sensation in her pelvis and legs, accompanied by jerky, involuntary pelvic movements. Barbara quickly stopped these movements by tensing her abdomen, legs, and pelvis.

In describing what she was experiencing, Barbara explained with astonishment that for the first time in three years, she was having clearly defined sexual feelings. Embarrassed, she said that she had consciously made herself tense to reduce her growing sexual excitement. Barbara then recognized that the abdominal pressure caused by her depression was always accompanied by pelvic tightness.

Barbara revealed that she came from an emotionally rigid family, in which sex was regarded as immoral and taboo. She was still living at home with her parents and had dated only one man for a brief period three years earlier. He had left her because of her sexual rigidity. Although Barbara had experienced sexual attraction for him, she had felt nothing similar since the relationship ended. In fact, this "lack of sexuality" (in her words) was her primary reason for seeking psychological help.

Despite Barbara's assertion that she wanted to experience sexual feelings, she found these sensations quite anxiety provoking. Whenever she began to feel sexually aroused, she would unconsciously tighten her pelvis, legs, and abdomen. This tightening would effectively stop movement and its accompanying sensation of arousal. The sensation which Barbara experienced as abdominal pressure reached consciousness as a feeling of emotional depression. By mislabeling her sexual feelings as "depression," Barbara was utilizing a psychological defense. Depression was for Barbara an acceptable emotion that she could discuss openly without becoming embarrassed.

By staying with her physical sensation instead of her mental interpretation of that sensation, Barbara came to be aware that she had severed herself from an important aspect of her life force. Once this awareness was strengthened intellectually and physically, Barbara could start accepting her sexuality as a definite part of herself and her life. After her realization in the therapeutic group, Barbara consciously chose to remain aware of the tightness she experienced when her sexual feelings returned. But now, for the first time, she allowed herself to feel pleasurable sexual sensations without resisting them.

Another patient I treated had a similar breakthrough. Jason, twenty-three, was a member of another therapeutic group I led. He was a pale, thin young man who worked as a musician. In his words, he wanted to "feel more alive." He complained of feeling awkward whenever he socialized. Although Jason described this problem during several previous sessions, he seemed to derive little benefit from the discussions. But during one session, he actually experienced the feeling of awkwardness he had been describing. At that moment, I asked him to describe what he was feeling physically and where in his body he was feeling it.

Jason answered that his entire body felt "tangled up." This was a familiar feeling to Jason. He explained to the group that he had previously tried to stop the sensation because he knew it was the physical counterpart to the anguish of emotional awkwardness. Most of the time, however, his attempts at physical untangling only heightened his feeling of inner awkwardness. On this occasion, I asked Jason not to try to untangle himself, but to remain as tangled up as possible and to experience himself fully that way.

While doing this, Jason began to feel shaky. He said that in the past, whenever his awkwardness intensified, he experienced this same kind of shakiness. Characteristically, he handled the uncomfortable sensation by leaving the social situation which was causing it and isolating himself. However, experiencing this shakiness now in our therapeutic group, Jason made no effort to run away. With encouragement from group members, he allowed the sensation of shakiness to fill his entire body.

As he did so, Jason's eyes—usually sad and dull—started sparkling. His pallor gave way to a healthy glow. He laughed and laughed. By not blocking spontaneity, Jason discovered his aliveness. Of course, this feeling of joy had been inside him all along, but because he unconsciously feared it as much as he sought it, Jason had called it "awkwardness." By thus mislabeling his aliveness, Jason never had to confront his accompanying fear. He could go on saying that he wanted to feel more alive while safely avoiding vibrant sensations. In that group moment, though, the pleasure that Jason felt in his "entangled awkwardness" was enough stimulus for him to begin facing and overcoming his fear.

I first learned about our tendency to mislabel feelings at one of Stanley Keleman's workshops, during which he treated Robert, a forty-two-year-old accountant who had come to regard himself as incapable of loving. Despite the fact that others viewed Robert as warm and emotionally giving, he himself felt little except frustration. "I feel nothing" was his depressing refrain.

Robert had tried all sorts of things to stimulate his

feelings, but nothing proved effective. Many well-meaning friends and well trained psychotherapists had tried to help Robert get in touch with his feelings. But like all the king's horses and men, they had failed in their efforts.

During this session, Keleman observed that Robert was in fact already feeling, because his sense of nothingness was a feeling—just as physical numbness is a distinct sensation. He instructed Robert to pay closer attention to his body and to describe the physical sensations that accompanied his feeling of nothingness. He asked Robert to focus on where in his body his bleak sensation was localized.

Robert was initially uncertain, but his puzzlement soon gave way to surprise and then to fright as he pointed to his chest. He spoke haltingly of a strange and frightening sensation there. His impulse was to stop the therapeutic session immediately, but with Keleman's gentle encouragement, Robert took the risk of allowing himself to experience his fear without fleeing from it.

Robert's fear intensified greatly, then gradually subsided as he maintained awareness of it. He began to speak excitedly about a delightful sense of warmth centered in his chest, which soon spread throughout his body. Then Robert's eyes filled with tears, and he cried unashamedly with his whole body.

Just as suddenly, Robert's body began to shake with laughter. He beamed joyfully at us and said, "I feel full of love." Of course, the love had been part of him all along, but it had frightened him because of its intensity. By mislabeling his feelings as "nothingness," Robert could numb himself and maintain control. All previous efforts by friends and therapists to get him "to feel," had inadvertently forced him only to strengthen his defensive self-numbing. By fully experiencing his inner resistance rather than suppressing it, Robert could discern his process of mislabeling clearly. Reconnected to his own love, Robert could cope more effectively with his remaining fears about intimacy.

## THE DANGER OF OVER-CONTROL

Getting in touch with our feelings and body sensations is crucial to developing self-worth. Conversely, cutting ourselves off from our bodies and the life energy that flows within is a sure way of stifling the development of self-worth. Quite simply, by subordinating our feelings to logic or by mislabeling them, we pay too high a price for staying on top of the situation. This is particularly important to understand because it is simultaneously possible to be in control and yet fully in touch with our emotions. Confusion arises only when we fail to distinguish adequately between feelings and actions.

Undoubtedly, if we had no inhibitions and acted out all our feelings, chaos would result. However, experiencing a feeling fully is by no means synonymous with acting on that feeling. The key issue is deciding what to do about a feeling, or to put it another way, deciding whether to use logic to determine our response. For instance, if someone makes us so angry that we feel like punching him, our logical mind may advise us that hitting is not in our best interest. We are then free to choose. Should we choose not to strike, we have neither suppressed our strong emotion nor denied our right to it. However, when our logical mind keeps us from even becoming aware of our angry impulse to retaliate we have no opportunity to choose.

Logic can be either a destructive or a constructive force in relation to our feelings. Rationality is harmful when it judges whether emerging feelings should even reach the level of conscious awareness. But rationality is helpful when it is employed to support or offset the pressure toward physical action that feelings often exert. Though it keeps us in control, using rationality to judge our emerging feelings delegitimizes our emotions and diminishes our vitality and self-worth. Using our reason to modify our physical responses, on the other hand, allows us full possession of our experience and actually enhances our self-worth.

## WALKING THE TIGHTROPE

Though I have clearly suggested that process is more important than goal, it is crucial to understand that an intense involvement with process is not necessarily a positive force. To understand this concept, imagine a skillful tightrope walker who dreams of becoming rich and famous. His opportunity finally comes when he is offered a huge sum of money and network television coverage to walk a tightrope stretched between two skyscrapers, with no safety net below him.

The tightrope walker chooses to risk his life for the sake of his goal. He thinks of the great reward until the moment he steps onto the rope. And riches and fame are his first thought when he completes his dangerous act. But while walking on the tightrope itself, the man never thinks of his reward. While balancing himself between the two skyscrapers, he concentrates completely on the process. Even a fleeting thought of his goal could prove fatal.

Here, then, is a man who is clearly impelled by a goal. But in its pursuit, he remains completely involved in the process of getting there. However, such an outlook in life is not entirely healthy. In essence, the tightrope walker resembles a businessman who through personal drive to reach the pinnacle of success devotes himself wholly to the process of "making it." For such individuals, the process has importance only as a tool: not as an experience meaningful in and of itself.

My point is that what helps us to develop self-worth is not mere involvement in the process, but the *nature* of that involvement. Is our involvement an obsession to succeed at a particular goal? Or is it a commitment to value each moment of life for its unique and precious qualities?

The sport of surfing provides another example of problems in this context. Surely, the purpose of surfing is not for the surfer to reach shore as quickly as possible. The graceful figure balancing on a surfboard with seeming ease is hardly saying to himself or herself, "I can't wait until I get to the beach!" Rather, it is as if the surfer has become one with the wave being ridden and the board that connects flesh and water. Such an image symbolizes true involvement in the moment.

However, even if the surfer is enjoying the process and is not intent on becoming the best surfer on the beach, he or she must be careful to remain detached from ego concerns during the surfing experience. Both reveling in pride and showing off ultimately lower our self-worth, because they cause us to depend on the approval of others for personal gratification.

A third way in which involvement in process can be distorted is by trying too hard. For example, it is self-defeating to "try to relax," since the effort inherent in trying stands in opposition to relaxation. When we try too hard, getting in touch with process ends up becoming just another goal. We must remember that it is in *being*, not *doing*, in letting go, that we experience process. The more we strain to live in the here and now, the more we undermine our actually being there.

There are many people who sincerely wish to become more involved in process, but defeat themselves repeatedly by working too hard at getting it right.

When they realize what they are doing, they are likely to say, "All right! I'll try not to do it anymore!" But this attitude merely perpetuates the struggle.

It is not always easy to get off the merry-go-round. The solution cannot come from assigning ourselves specific tasks. Instead, the best way that I know to learn to balance process and goal is to establish a relationship with another person who can serve as a role model and teach us not by saying, but by doing.

Such a teacher instructs the same way a parent helps a child walk. The parent creates a safe environment in which the child can learn. Even with such help, the journey will not be easy or short. Much time and patience will be required of both the teacher and the learner.

The film version of the *Wizard of Oz* has an amusing yet poignant scene that often guides me when I see people overpursuing goals in the hope of finding happiness. The scene takes place towards the end of the movie when, defrocked and with his back to the wall, the Wizard's true wisdom comes to the fore. He recognizes that at some level, each of the characters who sought something from him already possesses that which he or she sought. Utilizing this insight, the Wizard reaches into his "magic" bag and gives his three nonhuman petitioners—the scarecrow, lion, and tin man—symbols of what they most desire.

Because they are stuck in a goal oriented approach to life, these characters depend on external recognition to appreciate what is truly themselves. For example, to the scarecrow, happiness lies in having a brain. He is oblivious to all internal evidence that he already has a fine one; and so, his search for a brain focuses on externals. Seeing this, the Wizard awards the scarecrow a diploma that attests to his intellectual accomplishment. Believing in the diploma more than in himself, the scarecrow uses this award to allow himself to function "as if" he had a brain.

For Dorothy, the only human petitioner, the Wizard can find nothing suitable in his bag. Even his wondrous balloon, which he has been saving as a last resort, proves to be utterly useless for her. It is not uncommon during times of desperation for people to discover unforeseen strengths in themselves and initiate major changes in their outlook. Thus, Dorothy, cut off from what she perceives as her only source of help, learns that she already has within herself the power she has been seeking from others throughout her adventure. She needs only look inside herself, and she will at last be home in Kansas.

Medals, gold watches, and diplomas are all part of society's goal oriented illusion. After all, what would happen to the scarecrow's brain if his diploma were revoked? The truth that Dorothy comes to see is part of the process oriented solution to bringing joy and fulfillment to our daily lives.

So the question remains: how much of our lives is spent at the circus and how much is spent traveling there? Striking the proper balance between goal and process is a key to strengthening our sense of self-worth. We each have the ability to find that balance, whatever our age, social status, income level, or life circumstance.

# 4

# Putting the Giants to Sleep: What Meditation Does

*The days pass and are gone, and one finds that he never once had time to really think. . . . One who does not meditate cannot have wisdom.*

Rabbi Nachman of Bratslav

My interest in meditation as a tool for enhancing self-worth came about quite indirectly as a result of meeting several remarkable people in my travels around the globe. As I became acquainted with them and asked how they had attained their wisdom, they invariably cited the use of meditation. For example, in Russia I met a woman who was apparently able to move objects without touching them. When I inquired how she had come to possess this mysterious skill, she replied swiftly, "Through meditation."

Of course, I became intrigued. As I delved into the subject of meditation, I discovered that it is taught in many of the world's cultures and described in several venerated texts. I learned that comprehensive systems of meditation have flourished since the dawn of history. For example, the Hebrew Bible alludes to meditation as the method by which all prophets achieved visionary states of consciousness.

What is meditation really about? How does meditative practice relate to present knowledge about the human mind? Can we believe the apparently extravagant claims of its advocates? Are there dangers associated with meditation? To find answers to these questions, I did a lot of reading as well as some experiential investigation. I explored the forms of meditation practiced in a variety of spiritual traditions, including Christian, Jewish, Buddhist, Hindu, and Sufi. After nearly a decade of careful inquiry, I have come to understand and teach many aspects of meditation often neglected in popular books and courses.

Before I begin, I must make one vital point. Meditation is *not* another name for relaxation training. We may use meditative practice as a way to relax, but doing so is like using a sledge hammer to swat a fly. It can be done, but we expend a tremendous amount of energy to accomplish something we can do more easily. If we want to be more relaxed in our everyday lives—a worthwhile and important goal—we do not need to use such a potent technique as meditation. There are simpler methods that will produce equally restful results.

## WHAT IS MEDITATION?

As a psychiatrist interested in spiritual growth, I believe that each of us has within us many levels of consciousness. I have found that the best way to understand this notion is through the analogy of a skyscraper. Imagine yourself standing at the lobby entrance. The building soars one hundred stories above you. You know that by using the elevators, you can visit any of the one hundred floors.

Now, some people view meditation as a goal in itself: they meditate for the sake of meditating. There is nothing immoral or harmful about such an attitude. But this attitude is like traveling by train and taxi all the way to a famous skyscraper and then just sitting in the elevator! In so doing, we are not really using the elevator for its intended purpose of carrying people to the upper floors of the building to accomplish their business.

A state of deep inner relaxation might correspond to the skyscraper's first or second floor, but no higher. Using meditation to enter a restful emotional state is thus not very sensible. We could just as easily use the building's stairs to get to the first or second floor. We are almost wasting our time to ride the elevator up one flight, when it was designed to transport us skyward.

This analogy has an important message. Yet, I have found that even individuals who meditate regularly often seem to miss it. They have been told, perhaps by sincere and well-meaning teachers, that meditation will help them relax. To them meditative practice has become a kind of relaxation training. A major influence on this trend has been the work of Dr. Herbert Benson, a Harvard University medical researcher who became interested in meditation and its therapeutic uses. He explained in his book *The Relaxation Response* that meditation has proved to be an effective, healthful tool enabling many people to lower their blood pressure. However, Dr. Benson found that the particular meditative technique that people used did not influence these beneficial results. Rather, the meditative process itself was the key factor.

Dr. Benson's early research focused on the use of *mantra* techniques, in which the individual repeats aloud the same sound over and over. He concluded that the specific meditative sound repeated was unimportant. That is, his research subjects could lower their blood pressure just as effectively by focusing on the sound "one"—or presumably, even "Coca Cola"—as on some ancient phrase. Presumably, all that mattered was that for twenty consecutive minutes the individual repeated a neutral sound while exhaling. The result was a highly beneficial physiological state in which blood pressure dropped and other healthful changes occurred.

Dr. Benson's research created a real problem for those interested in meditation. For thousands of years, our great spiritual traditions have taught that the particular meditative method one uses is vitally important, yet Benson's research clearly suggests that the choice is not significant at all. Can this seeming contradiction be reconciled?

Let us return once more to the analogy of the skyscraper and the elevator. In my view, Dr. Benson was looking only at the first or second floor of the building and asking: Which meditative system will transport us there? Not surprisingly, he verified that they all do. Every meditative technique produces a state of deep relaxation, with lowered blood pressure and pulse rate. Presumably the world's spiritual masters would agree with this finding. But all might also legitimately insist: Our meditative methods are designed to carry individuals much higher—to the tenth, or fiftieth, or one-hundredth floor. We are interested in going far beyond the first floor!*

If we bear this analogy in mind, the nature of meditation becomes more comprehensible. Seeking deep relaxation and seeking lofty inner states of consciousness are entirely separate goals. There is nothing wrong

*In *Beyond the Relaxation Response* (1984), Benson does recognize the importance of what he calls "the Faith Factor."—ED.

with wanting to lower our blood pressure or pulse rate, but historically meditative practices have never been intended or utilized for such relatively mundane objectives.

## LEVELS OF CONSCIOUSNESS

Before proceeding, it may be useful to ask: what do we really mean by the term "consciousness"? What does the phrase "levels of consciousness" imply?

First, is of course, the state of consciousness that we normally experience when we are awake. We are intimately familiar with that one. We also know that our waking consciousness is clearly different from our awareness while we are sleeping. Thus we recognize already two kinds of consciousness—for certainly, sleep involves mental activity such as dreams, images, and thought fragments. During sleep, something is definitely happening within us, but in sleep, consciousness is clearly a state different from the waking state.

Other states of consciousness also manifest in everyday life. One of these is the wondrous state called love. Can you think back to your first romantic encounter? Or, if you are a parent, can you recall the day your first child was born? Undoubtedly, the event changed everything around you, and altered the way the world looked. When you felt that surge of love, a new state of consciousness was born inside you, through which you saw and experienced everything differently.

There are other inner states in which people typically perform extraordinary and even seemingly impossible actions. I remember a newspaper story in New York City about a young mother who lifted an automobile to save her screaming toddler who was trapped underneath the wheels. The child was in danger of being crushed. Somehow, without thinking, the mother dashed over and lifted the car to save her daughter's life. There were witnesses; these kinds of events really do occur. More recently, a radio station broadcast a news report about a construction worker who lifted a two-ton cement beam to save a fellow worker being crushed beneath it.

In these instances and in countless others, the heroic person is operating from a dramatically different state of consciousness. If we say to the mother or the construction worker the following day, "Okay, let's see you lift this car or cement beam. You did it yesterday, didn't you?" it seems obvious that they would fail. In our ordinary state of consciousness, such feats are unthinkable. But there is a way of being in the world in which such actions are possible. For instance, Asian martial arts which rely on meditation have taught for millennia how to cultivate inward states which release superhuman strength and endurance.

It is clear that we can control some inner states of awareness, such as whether to fall asleep or not. But some internal states lie beyond our ordinary, conscious control. For example, suppose you are sitting in a classroom feeling physically quite tired. Though you are interested in the speaker's topic, your mind is beginning to wander. Outwardly, you are actively listening to the lecturer, but you suddenly realize that you have been daydreaming and have missed her last few remarks.

You deliberately refocus your attention. But after a few minutes you realize that you have been daydreaming again, perhaps fantasizing pleasantly about the attractive person in the front row, worrying about some overdue bills, or mentally replaying an unresolved dispute with a coworker that took place earlier in the week.

Thus, daydreaming is another state of consciousness.

Though you really want to absorb the lecture, your mind does not obey you. You can hear the speaker, but you can not quite tune in to her words. Although you are physically present in the room, mentally you are somewhere else. Sometimes, we can control our daydreaming consciousness. We can decide whether to listen to the speaker or to fantasize about the person in the front row. Often, however, we are unable to control this mental state. We may struggle with great effort to stay alert and yet repeatedly find that our daydreams take over.

Another relatively familiar state of consciousness involves hypnosis. If you are a receptive subject, your normal waking state will be radically altered by hypnotic induction. Psychological researchers have verified that under hypnosis some people can recall seemingly forgotten pieces of information like the names of their first grade teacher and classmates. As you now read these words, such information is probably inaccessible to your consciousness. But hypnosis can awaken such memories. Police departments routinely employ psychologists trained in hypnosis to help crime victims recall details vanished from their ordinary consciousness. Thus, even though we cannot voluntarily enter the hypnotic state, we can choose to be put under hypnosis.

A less obvious example of the hypnotic state takes place when we watch a movie in a theatre. Whenever we find ourselves emotionally affected by the action on screen—feeling tense or fearful, crying or laughing—we have to some degree become hypnotized. We have allowed the movie's flickering images to become real to us. On one level of reality, we are simply sitting on a cushioned chair in a large darkened room. But on another level, we are emotionally involved with the drama being enacted on the screen. Psychologists have learned that the physical act of raising our eyes slightly to look at an image above us, like a movie on a raised screen, seems to induce a hypnotic state more readily.

In short, we experience several states of consciousness over the course of our everyday lives. Meditation is a method which enables us to attain states of consciousness less familiar to us, but with potentially great inner rewards.

## NURTURING OUR SPIRITUAL BODY

Earlier, I presented the idea that we are comprised of body, mind, and spirit. Stated so tersely, this idea seems an oversimplification, but it is nevertheless helpful in guiding our understanding of meditation. If we conceptualize these three parts of ourselves as separate but interrelated bodies, then we can meaningfully say that every individual has a physical body, a mental body, and a spiritual body.

Each of our three bodies develops in proportion to the care and attention we devote to it. For instance, even if we do not engage in a daily or weekly regimen of physical exercise, we still brush our hair, bathe and dress ourselves, and perform many other activities that involve us with our physical body every day. The same is true for our mental body. We know that our minds are active throughout the day, and that we are highly involved with our stream of thoughts.

But for the most part, this pattern of regular daily care does not hold true for our spiritual body. We typically accord it little or even no attention in the course of day-to-day living. Often, we give it virtually no attention whatsoever. For instance, consider a person who meditates an hour every day. This seems like a lot of spiritual activity. But are there not twenty-three additional hours at one's daily disposal? Yet, few of us in contemporary Western civilization devote even as much as one hour a day to caring for our spiritual body. As a result, most of us possess—in relative terms, of course—a gigantic physical body, a gigantic mental body and a miniscule spiritual body.

To extend this analogy further, it is reasonable to conjecture that our huge physical and mental bodies have powerful, booming voices, and that our spiritual body has a correspondingly weak, tiny voice. Now, if you imagine that all three are speaking to you simultaneously, what is the likelihood of your hearing the tiny voice of your miniscule spiritual body? Unfortunately, this scenario rather accurately describes the situation of most people in our culture.

It is hardly surprising, consequently, that many people claim sincerely, "I go occasionally to church or synagogue. But I feel almost nothing. I just can't seem to connect with anything that could be called spiritual. I read books that describe uplifting experiences, but when I try spiritual activities, nothing seems to happen. Maybe, spirituality is just an imaginary way to make us feel better about life."

Such an attitude is very common today. Yet, if we recall our analogy of the three bodies, how can we be aware of our spiritual experience if our two powerful voices are booming and we are trying to hear the tiny voice? Our gigantic mental and physical bodies command too much of our attention.

This analogy yields one useful way to understand the meditative process: Meditation is a time-honored and effective way of "putting the giants to sleep." That is our goal in a nutshell. We do not want to kill or cripple the giants, because we need our physical and mental capabilities. How could we function everyday without our physical perceptions and our mental thoughts? Indeed, we must treat the giants with loving-kindness if we are to lead happy, productive lives.

As a physician, I further believe that we need to improve the care we give to our giants. That issue is addressed in later chapters. But in speaking about meditation here, I am suggesting that it would be nice if the giants could nap once in a while. If they are quiet and not snoring, we can hear our small spiritual voice far more clearly. Only when we successfully put the giants to sleep will the neglected voice of spirituality become real to us, instead of being something exotic to read about in books.

How can we hear what our spiritual body is saying? The answer is quite simply by meditating. Meditation is a specific technique to accomplish the goal of transporting us to the higher floors in the skyscraper of our being. Of course, we must first know which buttons to push. If we step into the elevator and start pressing buttons randomly, we are unlikely to get to our desired destination.

In this context, there is a fascinating story about aviator Charles Lindbergh and his daring solo flight across the Atlantic Ocean in the 1920s. The story comes from Lindbergh's diary. At a particular moment after many sleepless hours, Lindbergh noted that he was feeling tremendous emotional tension. Suddenly he experienced extreme drowsiness. Lindbergh wrote, "Shaking my body and stamping my feet no longer has effect. It's more fatiguing than arousing. I'll have to try something else."

His flight log, *The Spirit of St. Louis*, records what Lindbergh did next:

> I push the stick forward and dive down into a high ridge of cloud, pulling up sharply after I clip through

> its summit. That wakes me a little, but tricks don't help for long.
>
> My eyes close, and open, and close again. But I'm beginning to understand vaguely a new factor which has come to my assistance. It seems I'm made up of three personalities. . . . There's my body, which knows definitely that what it wants most in the world is sleep. There's my mind, constantly making decisions that my body refuses to comply with, but which itself is weakening in resolution. And there's something else, which seems to become stronger instead of weaker with fatigue, an element of spirit, a directive force, that has stepped out from the background and taken control over both mind and body. It seems to guard them as a wise father guards his children; letting them venture to the point of danger, then calling them back, guiding with a firm but tolerant hand. (p. 361)

Lindbergh's experience over the Atlantic illustrates my point about the three parts of our human makeup. Interestingly, he arrived at his important insight by exhausting his body and mind totally. For many centuries this method has been taught as a way to allow the human spiritual body to express itself more fully. Any of us can do it. We do not need to fly solo across the ocean. But, if we, like Lindbergh, place ourselves under unrelenting pressure—until we feel physically and emotionally depleted—one of two things will happen.

As our mind and body become progressively weaker, we might experience a debilitating breakdown. When this happens our spiritual body is still overwhelmed by our other two bodies. If, however, we have the inner strength and fortitude of someone like Charles Lindbergh, we may, in this exhausted state, begin to discern another part of ourselves, perhaps for the first time.

If Lindbergh's method were the only way to hear

our inner voice, spiritual growth would be a very dangerous endeavor. Fortunately, many less hazardous methods exist. But the awakening of the spirit that Lindbergh experienced has been recognized as a spiritual technique for centuries. Intense stress and fatigue can temporarily weaken the mental and physical bodies sufficiently for the voice of our spiritual body to be heard.

Meditation offers a safer and more controlled way of strengthening our spiritual body. To be sure, meditative practices are not without their own risks; the Kabbalah, the esoteric branch of Judaism, is quite clear about this. But if we understand these risks beforehand, we are likely to be guided safely in our practice. The end point of all meditative efforts is the same state that Lindbergh experienced—a state in which we have put our physical and mental bodies to sleep.

Putting the physical body to sleep is certainly not very difficult. We do it every night when we go to bed. But putting our physical body to sleep while we are still in a waking state—that can be tricky. During meditation, we must also put our mind to sleep, but at the same time, retain full awareness of what is taking place.

Remember for a moment the parable of the man and the tree in Chapter 2 and its relation to meditative practice. What in fact are we trying to grow? For most of us our spiritual body is still a tiny seed. We are seeking to make that miniscule form larger and more powerful. Certainly, if we understood the manifold principles of biology, we could understand how and why a tree grows. In the same way, if we understand spiritual biology, we can see how a particular meditative technique will help our spiritual body to blossom. Our problem is that since we do not have higher spiritual awareness to begin with, we cannot discern clearly what the meditative exercise is trying to accomplish. That is our dilemma.

Initially, therefore, it is possible that the meditative exercises described in Chapter 6 will make about as much sense to you as pouring water on bare ground. But I feel sure that if you practice these techniques faithfully and patiently, you will eventually experience enhanced self-worth.

## LEARNING TO KEEP STILL

In the next chapter, we explore a variety of meditative methods designed to strengthen the spiritual self. But to start, the first thing I recommend is that you work on putting your physical body to sleep while you are still mentally awake. When you have accomplished that, we can talk about the next step—putting your mind to sleep as well.

So we begin with the body. The first step is simply to sit for a period of time without moving. What could be easier? It sounds absurdly easy—just sit still without moving your body for a set period of time. However, it is likely that none of the instructions I give in the rest of this book will be more demanding or challenging.

You should be aware that sitting still without moving is *not* meditation—it is simply a prelude or first step—a way to put the physical body to sleep. When you can consistently succeed in putting your mind and body to sleep *while you are still awake*, then you will really be meditating. You will be in the skyscraper's elevator, traveling to the upper floors of the building.

I recommend that you begin your practice with just a short period of time, so that you do not become frustrated and give up. Gradually, you will be able to build up the time you devote to sitting practice. What is the end point? To be able to sit still indefinitely. In practical terms, this means that when you have mastered keeping still, you will feel no strain in doing it. You can just as easily sit still for five hours as for five minutes. Many well-documented accounts confirm that accomplished meditators can do this.

Your task is not to accomplish this goal through grim willpower, but to attain it naturally, as easily as closing your eyes and falling asleep. We all know the pleasant experience of going to bed in an exhausted state, and then waking up refreshed what seems like moments later and finding that many hours have passed.

Similarly, when you can look forward to your sitting practice with eagerness, because it is so revitalizing—when there is no pain or discomfort—you will have mastered step one. When you have achieved this state, you are ready to move on to gaining control over your mind.

You may find along the way that you reap a multitude of physical benefits or even gain abilities that seem superhuman. Many of the incredible powers associated with yoga occur at this stage: yogis who can slow down or accelerate their heartbeat, or who need only a minimum of air to breathe, or a host of other seemingly miraculous powers. Yogis achieve this exquisite control over their body through sustained practice, based initially on learning to sit still.

Now, for those of you who have busy schedules and many activities to do each day, my recommendation that you simply sit still will doubtless seem strange. You will probably insist, "I have this to do, and that to do, and this to do, and I'm supposed to just sit there?!"

Yet, that is precisely what I am encouraging you to do. Your initial difficulties may be horrendous. You may experience physical obstacles, but these are often nothing as compared to your mental reactions. Meditation instructions are always deceptively simple. They must be, if the meditation is to be meaningful, because meditation generally involves doing just one thing. It is in the stopping of everything else that our difficulty arises.

In our fast-paced and increasingly frenzied culture, people have become accustomed to performing several actions simultaneously—driving their car while listening to the radio and thinking about work. Or, eating dinner while reading the newspaper or watching television and chatting with family members. Or camping in the mountains while using a portable computer and cellular telephone. That is why meditation is so challenging for many people in our culture, and also why it is so vital.

In all traditional Eastern meditative practices, ranging from archery to flower arranging to the tea ceremony, the essence is that we focus on doing one thing totally, in each moment. Here too the *process* and not the *goal* is crucial to our inner growth.

# 5

# How to Meditate

*To feel the whole in every part.*
M. C. Richards

Before starting meditative practice, we should recognize that all forms of meditation involve discipline, whatever their particular cultural or religious background. Indeed, the idea of discipline is crucial to the entire meditative process. This fact already presents a challenge to Americans, since our society discourages sustained, devoted, and patient effort in most endeavors. Meditation, in fact, requires a particular type of discipline with which few of us are familiar.

Discipline, of course, has a variety of connotations. For instance, the physical discipline needed to master a tennis swing involves learning a highly coordinated, directed set of body motions that are hardly innate. Or consider the processes of learning to ride a bicycle, swim, bake a pie, or drive an automobile. These are all relatively commonplace skills in our society that necessitate physical discipline.

But suppose we are asked, "Can you discipline your blood pressure or body temperature?" Undoubtedly, most of us would be confused by the very question. Why? Because such discipline requires a sophisticated *internal* body awareness, a skill with which few in American society have systematic experience. Our society encourages us to pay virtually no attention to inner body states. For this reason, meditation is often initially difficult, since it is more an internally-oriented than an externally-oriented discipline.

Now, consider what is involved in mental discipline. Most of us are familiar with applying our minds for hours to projects that interest us. Even though other potentially alluring activities may be available at the moment, we can usually exert the mental discipline necessary to complete our task. In our technological society, we are also relatively skilled at directing our minds toward writing or typing, reading material, or performing job-related paperwork.

But meditation requires another, unique kind of mental discipline. We must actually learn to control our thoughts. This is very different from other forms of directed mental activity. Just as most Americans are unfamiliar with the idea, let alone the practice, of controlling functions such as heart rate, or blood pressure, so too are they unfamiliar with the mental discipline required to regulate their thoughts. Even if Americans are well disciplined in many aspects of everyday life, we may lack the specific discipline required for effective meditation.

I cannot overemphasize the importance of self-discipline in meditation. Yet, strikingly, this is an issue that many would-be practitioners typically minimize or even neglect altogether. Somehow, they have acquired the erroneous notion that meditating—perhaps because it involves no external tools—is as easy to master as walking or eating. Few individuals would bother responding to a newspaper announcement saying something like: "Do you want to become a neurosurgeon? Come to a weekend course, and for $100 you can start studying neurosurgery!" Such an advertisement would strike almost all of us as either a fraud or an absurd joke. Yet, newspaper announcements about classes in meditation and healing generally produce a deluge of inquiries from persons expecting to acquire virtuosity in these ancient disciplines overnight.

In point of fact, it is far easier to become a neurosurgeon than to become a master of esoteric disciplines. How is this possible? Because if we wish to work as a neurosurgeon, we must simply follow a rather cut-and-dried academic process. First we must complete a structured sequence of college and medical school courses, and then complete supervised training and internship. So long as we have the necessary intellectual proficiency and manual dexterity, after ten or twelve years, we will gain the acumen needed to practice as a neurosurgeon.

But no cut-and-dried, formalized structure can help us pursue the skill of meditation. We can spend years in spiritual practice and still not attain true meditative mastery. Indeed, we may find ourselves still novices. Achieving meditative mastery is thus more open-ended than going to college and medical school. Becoming a neurosurgeon may require great intellectual discipline. But becoming a master of meditation and healing requires tremendous emotional, spiritual, and even physical discipline.

So should we give up trying to learn meditation before we even start? Of course not. I am not suggesting such a decision at all. But I would be remiss if I failed to stress that discipline is necessary if we are to reap the benefits of meditative practice. How do we develop such discipline? Isn't this why we need to meditate in the first place—to become more focused in our thoughts and desires?

A ready answer becomes powerfully vivid to me whenever I look at a baby learning to walk. The determination and courage that very young children exhibit in this struggle should instill us with awe. For your own benefit, watch this process sometime. See how many times the baby falls and perhaps cries, and yet rises up only to fall and cry again. The baby keeps at the task, never giving up the effort until it finally learns to walk. Eventually, of course, the child walks effortlessly.

I have often asked myself: how many of us, given a similar task during adulthood, would have the same determination to triumph over countless moments of frustration? I know very few individuals who have brought that much concerted effort and dedication to anything in their adult lives.

And yet, what we were once capable of as children, we are certainly capable of now. When we were young, our minds were less cluttered with trivia and irrelevant concerns. During adulthood, our mental set acts as our main obstacle to inner growth. Nevertheless, the ability to make a firm commitment to spiritual growth still resides in each of us. This is why the example of the baby learning to walk is so important to our discussion of meditative practice. If it helps, you may even wish to put up a picture of a baby learning to walk. Whenever you feel frustrated in your effort to enhance your self-worth, you should keep this model of determined effort in mind.

## SETTING A MEDITATIVE REGIMEN

When you first start to meditate, choose an amount of time that is realistic for you. A too lengthy session can be self-defeating. Generally speaking, you should begin with sessions lasting between five and ten minutes. Be specific, though, as to precisely how many minutes your first few sessions will be. As meditating becomes easier, you can increase the length of the sessions.

For example, suppose that you decide to practice meditation A for five minutes once a day. Initially, you may find it difficult to concentrate for even five consecutive minutes. But with regular daily practice, you will reach a point in which meditation has become relatively easy for that time period.

Now, you are ready to increase the time. You might consider adding five additional minutes to each session, each week. However, the specific number of minutes and the number of days or weeks between increments can be individualized. For instance, you may decide to meditate five minutes per session during the first week, ten minutes during the second, fifteen minutes during the third, and twenty minutes during the fourth. Or, you may choose to proceed more slowly, and meditate for five minutes per session during the first two weeks, ten minutes during the third and fourth weeks, and fifteen minutes during the fifth and sixth weeks. The important issue is that you feel comfortable with the time you have allotted.

Typically, it is desirable to meditate for twenty to thirty minutes in one session. This figure has no special, sacred significance, but it does represent a considerable chunk of daily time for most of us. This fact is important because we will get out of meditation exactly what we put into it. Interestingly, there is recent scientific evidence from the field of neurophysiology that certain circuits in the human brain need to be stimulated for at least twenty minutes before long-lasting effects result.

To be honest, the need for this twenty to thirty minute commitment produces the most common complaint that I hear in relation to meditation: "I just don't have the time. How can I possibly give up a half hour each day? Do you have any idea what my day is like? I don't have five free minutes, let alone twenty-five! I'd love to do it, but I just can't afford the time."

My usual response to this attitude is to point out what a crazy lifestyle a person must be leading if he or she cannot find even half an hour a day to devote to personal needs. Such a frenzied lifestyle already negates our self-worth. The first step to overcoming this no-win situation is to restructure our priorities so that we can set aside time each day for self-development. Indeed, for many individuals, setting aside such time is itself a way to enhance self-worth.

Besides the actual time you set aside for meditation you will benefit from reserving an additional one to five minutes as a transition period between the end of meditation and the resumption of your other activities. This allows you to shift your consciousness more gradually from the meditative to the nonmeditative state, just as a transition period between waking up in the morning and starting work is helpful. The amount of transition time needed varies with each individual and can best be determined through personal experience.

Although it is not crucial that you allot the same time each day for meditation—for instance, 8:00 to 8:30 A.M.—it is generally advantageous to set aside a specified daily time slot. Because we are all creatures of habit, it is easy to tell ourselves, "I'll do it later." Soon we are exhausted and ready for bed, with no time left to meditate. To break this habit, we must resolve that no matter how tired we are or how late the hour, we will not go to bed until we meditate. When it becomes clear to our body and mind that we are firm in our resolve, these "giants" will give up this ploy and seek other ways of stopping us.

The best time of day for meditation will likewise vary with the individual. In my experience, most people find mornings the best time for meditative practice. Of course, some people prefer afternoons or evenings, and I even know some who routinely awaken in the middle of the night to meditate, because they have found this time most effective. I encourage you to experiment in this regard, for meditating during your optimal time will enhance your experience and accelerate your inner growth.

However, if something happens on a given day to keep you from meditating at your best time, then by all means meditate at a different hour. Do not skip meditation completely. If you do, you are apt to discover quickly how many distracting things can "coincidentally" happen to interfere with your appointed meditation time.

Even after you have established a best time for daily meditation—and can do so regularly with ease—there is reason to meditate periodically at other times. Why? Because just as we tend to become hungry at our normal eating times, we may find that we automatically begin to enter a meditative state as we approach our regular hour for meditation. Although this automatic response may make it easier to meditate, it also indicates that we are not completely in control of the meditative state. In extreme cases, some individuals may unconsciously shift into a meditative inner state regardless of what they are doing at the time. This shift is akin to responding subliminally to a posthypnotic suggestion and represents one of the dangers inherent in meditation. If this starts happening to you, I recommend that you do not meditate regularly at a fixed time each day.

Even if you do not experience these specific difficulties, it is advisable that you meditate periodically at a time other than your usual one. Self-worth is enhanced by a sense of true control and direction. However, self-worth is less likely to increase if you feel dependent on a particular time of day to experience the benefits of meditation.

The same principle should guide you in other matters associated with meditative practice. For example, you may meditate best while sitting in a particular room or armchair, or while burning incense, or after turning off the lights. Each of these factors is part of a ritual that can facilitate meditation. There is certainly nothing intrinsically wrong with rituals. However, when such patterns are established in an unthinking, conditioned way, they can have a negative rather than a positive effect. So if you find yourself developing an attachment to meditating in a particular room or armchair, you should meditate periodically in another setting. In this way, you can make sure that your meditative state is independent of external factors and emanates from your own inner being.

An inexpensive instrument that can enhance your meditation is a book to use as a personal diary or log. Its purpose is to help you keep a systematic written record of your meditative experiences. Generally, the simpler your diary, the more likely you will be to maintain it daily.

After you meditate, make an entry with the following information: date, time of day, specific meditation practiced, and a comment about the session. Each of these items can be entered in a separate column on your diary page. Your comment should include what you felt during the meditation and whether you experienced any special insights, ideas, or problems.

For example, you might record: "July 28th; 8:00 to 8:30 P.M.; breathing meditation #1. Comment: Felt very energized after a few minutes and was able to keep focused on my breath with few distracting thoughts. These mostly concerned deadline pressures at work. When I finished the meditation, I had a strong urge to do more writing at home on my novel."

Keeping a meditation diary can greatly accelerate your inner growth. For one thing, the activity reinforces the discipline involved in meditating each day. It means that besides the meditation itself, you are devoting time regularly to thinking about your experience. Such sustained self-examination can enhance the clarity of your thinking. A diary is also a valuable tool for observing your particular patterns of growth. However, you may not be able to appreciate this pattern until several months have elapsed. Often the most important thing about keeping a meditation diary is the increased self-awareness and self-understanding that results.

It is more likely that you will write in your diary daily if the book you use has meaning for you. I therefore recommend that you choose a book that reflects your present values. If you tend to value expensive things, then buy an expensive book. If you prize pretty things, then get a book that you find aesthetically pleasing. Or, if you value things that you fashion yourself, then make a book for yourself. Whatever book you decide on, dedicate it exclusively to use as a meditation diary, and read through it periodically.

## THE METHOD IS ONLY A METHOD

There are many forms of meditation, even within a spiritual tradition such as Judaism, Christianity, Sufism, Buddhism, Hinduism, or Taoism. Some meditative techniques stress visualization; others rely on chanting; still others incorporate altered breathing or body postures. Despite these differences, virtually all spiritual systems insist that to enhance self-worth, you perform the particular method correctly. And yet, too much reliance upon technique can be self-defeating. There is a beautiful Sufi story that speaks to this issue.

Once a Sufi master named Ibrahim was walking on the beach beside a large lake. Suddenly, he heard the sound of a young man's voice, chanting a well-known meditative prayer. The chant seemed to come from across the lake. As it continued, the Sufi sage became impressed with the sincerity in the man's voice.

However, Ibrahim also realized that the young man was chanting the prayer incorrectly. His pronunciation was wrong on several words, and he was reversing the sequence of several phrases. Moved by the young man's obvious sincerity and devotion, the master decided to find the young man and teach him the right way to say the prayer.

So the Sufi master found a rowboat and rowed across the lake. When he arrived at the other side, he found a young fisherman sitting by the shore and chanting the prayer over and over. Ibrahim approached the man and introduced himself. The fisherman was awe-struck. He could hardly believe that before his eyes stood a renowned Sufi master. It seemed like a dream come true!

The Sufi sage sat patiently with the fisherman and taught him the correct pronunciation and phrasing of the prayer. Since he was nervous and struggling to learn correctly, the young man made many mistakes. However, he was so dedicated to praying the right way that he kept begging the master to spend a little more time with him.

Ibrahim was exceedingly patient and kind, and finally he felt that the fisherman had learned the prayer. The two men said goodbye, and the Sufi master returned to his rowboat and began rowing back across the lake. As he rowed, he recalled his own youthful zealousness and his yearning to pray in the right way. He remembered that his teachers long ago had told him about the vast power that can be tapped if one prays correctly.

With a nostalgic smile, Ibrahim dipped his oar into the water once more as the shoreline neared. Suddenly, he heard a noise and looked up from his dreamy state. Several yards away, he saw the young fisherman running across the lake, trying to catch up with the rowboat. Breathless, he made a leap and reached the Sufi sage. In an imploring voice, the fisherman exclaimed, "Please, O master, tell me one more time how to say the prayer! Forgive me! I have forgotten the right way to say it!"

So what is the right way to meditate? Down through the centuries, spiritual traditions have taught various meditative techniques to serve as guideposts and to provide direction in our lives. But we must never believe that there is a single way that works for everyone. Nor should we be rigid in the application of each specific meditation. Ultimately only three rules are relevant. Each can help us combat our physical and mental giants.

## OUTWITTING THE GIANTS: THREE CARDINAL RULES

1. *Choose a particular meditation, and stay with it.*

This guideline is very important. Yet, I am amazed at how rarely it is mentioned in discussions of meditative practice. Thus far, we have not explored specific techniques of meditation, but these are discussed in Chapter 6. After reading them, you may sit down one day and say to yourself, "Okay, I want to practice meditation #1."

You start the meditation, but after a few minutes, you will almost certainly decide that you have made the wrong choice—that it really would be much better for your inner growth if you practiced meditation #2. And, indeed you may be totally correct. Meditation #2 may be more productive for you at this time. But the crucial rule here is: Do not switch!

Stay with your original meditation, no matter how keenly you yearn for a different one. Why? Because I guarantee that once you allow yourself to switch, no sooner will you start meditation #2 then you will decide that meditation #3 is even better. And, when you switch to meditation #3, you will decide that meditation #1 was actually the best one after all. By now, your meditation session will be in complete chaos.

My point is not that you are stuck with meditation #1 for the rest of your life, but rather, that you stay committed to one technique for a particular period of time. If you have contracted with yourself to practice meditation #1 for two weeks, then keep your agreement, and do not switch to another one until the appropriate date.

2. *Choose a time period for your meditation session before you meditate, and stick with it.*

I usually advise using a timer, such as an inexpensive kitchen device, to keep track of time during meditation. You can certainly glance periodically at a nearby clock to see how much time has passed. However, this method has the obvious disadvantage of interrupting your meditative concentration with irrelevant thoughts and actions.

Two disadvantages of a timer are its ticking and its ringing, but both of these can be circumvented easily. I advise that you muffle the ticking by placing the timer under a pillow, in a drawer, or even in another room. To avoid being startled by a loud, irritating ring, either muffle the timer or get one with a soft, pleasant chime.

In fact, the human body has an exquisitely accurate built-in clock, capable of measuring the passage of time precisely. This biological tool lets people wake themselves up at a predetermined hour. Or, they can conduct time-limited activities without having to keep track of the passing minutes. For those who have already developed this useful inner tool, I suggest that you practice using it first in other aspects of daily life—such as getting up in the morning at a given time—before you apply it to meditation.

3. *Contract with yourself how often you will meditate and keep to your contract.*

You may decide to meditate once a day, or once a week, or three times a day. But once you establish a pattern of frequency for your meditative practice, keep to it. Do not say to yourself, "Well, today really isn't a good day. I'm too tense, or tired, or excited to meditate."

These are the three cardinal rules for effective meditation, and they are absolutely essential. What is their rationale? Remember that in Chapter 4 we discussed our physical and mental bodies, and said that they resemble giants in comparison to our tiny spiritual body? I emphasized that for most of us, these giants have huge, booming voices, whereas our spiritual voice is barely audible. I also suggested that in order for us to hear the soft but important inner voice, we must put the giants to sleep.

Now, though these giants are big, they are not fools. Our physical and mental giants are very crafty, especially the mental giant, who has many clever tricks up its proverbial sleeve.

What do I mean? When you begin meditating, you

are saying to the mental giant in effect: "All right! Go to sleep, so that my spiritual body can come speak more loudly."

Do you really think your mental giant is going to obey? In this context, the film *2001* provides a relevant analogy. In it, several astronauts are on a spaceship hurtling toward Jupiter. Because it is a long journey, the spaceship is controlled by a computer named "Hal" that plays chess, talks to the astronauts, and exhibits other varied capabilities. One day one of the astronauts realizes that Hal has made an error and therefore can no longer be trusted to control the spaceship. He decides that Hal must immediately be shut off. The astronaut must alert the others on board, but he cannot tell them without Hal overhearing the plan and preventing the astronauts from assuming manual command of the spaceship.

Bearing this analogy in mind, let us return to the question of how to meditate effectively. At this moment, your conscious mind is reviewing everything you are reading here. For instance, it is reviewing how you plan to maneuver around it, and it is sarcastically saying to itself, "Oh yeah?" It knows all about your desire for self-development, and it is thinking, "You fool! Do you expect that I'm going to give up control and let you put me to sleep?"

In short, there is no way that you can tell yourself or anyone else how you will maneuver around the mental giant without its hearing, objecting, and seeking to thwart you.

That is our dilemma. The question is: how *do* we get beyond the conscious mind? The answer is: we must not let the mental giant ever serve as the decision maker about meditation. If we do, our mental giant will say quite reasonably, as we meditate, "Look, rules don't really count. Even your book said so, with that story about the fisherman and the Sufi master. Forget the timer! Just sit for however long feels right. The whole idea is to get in touch with yourself, anyway, isn't it? So what do you need the timer for? Forget the timer."

Who do you think is going to decide what feels right? Who do you think is going to make you feel restless or bored? And, what do you think that the discomfort you may experience really indicates? Given free reign, our mental giant will persuade us to abandon the meditation as soon as it starts to feel a little shaky, a little less in control. After precisely ten minutes, for example, you might say to yourself, "Boy, this has been a good meditation, so I'll stop now. I really feel relaxed!" Why will your mind tell you this? Because the mental giant knows that *after* more than ten minutes, it will start to feel shaky. The next day, you may decide to sit for longer—perhaps fifteen or even twenty minutes. On this occasion your mental giant is allowing you to sit longer. Perhaps, it hopes you will fail and give up meditating altogether.

So as silly as these three rules may seem, they are absolutely necessary. The only way to wrest control from your mental giant is to establish the length of your meditation session *in advance.*

Why do you need a contract? The same rationale applies. Say you are using meditation #1, and it does not threaten your conscious mind. Your mental giant can let you perform that meditation for the next thirty years, for all it cares. But suppose meditation #1 is proving effective in strengthening your spiritual body and amplifying its voice. Your ego will immediately feel threatened and will therefore say, seemingly innocently but actually quite cunningly, "Why don't you try meditation #2? Meditation #1 is boring! It won't accomplish anything. With #1, you're just wasting your time. Come on, switch to meditation #2. It's much better!" Your mental giant will provide all sorts of rational sounding reasons for switching, and you will be tricked into going along. Perhaps, you will switch to meditation #3, which your ego can counteract more easily.

Finally, the same argument applies to the frequency of your meditation practice. Make a contract with yourself *before* you start to meditate, whether you decide to practice once a day, twice a day, or whatever frequency you choose. Once you begin, you will struggle with your conscious mind over how often you sit, just as you struggled over the issues of technique and time. Here too, the only chance you have of succeeding with meditation is to make decisions beforehand.

Our struggle with our mental giant is very much like the evocative Greek legend of the Sirens in Homer's *Odyssey:* whenever the captain of a ship would hear the seductively beautiful songs the Sirens would sing, he would forget to steer the ship. It would crash against the rocks, and all on board would drown. Knowing full well that the Sirens would be irresistible, Ulysses warned his crew: "Tie me to the mast before we reach the Sirens. Then, no matter what I say, no matter how much I plead or threaten, do not listen to me until we have passed their point." This was the only way Ulysses could navigate the ship safely past the Sirens.

Of course, you have chosen to read this book with the cooperation of your conscious mind. But your motivation may stem partially from curiosity and partially from an intellectual openness to experiencing new things. Consequently, you should be aware that the moment your mental giant feels its power threatened, it will fight back with clever stratagems. That is what the struggle for inner growth is all about.

The story of Ulysses reminds me of another provocative analogy about our inner makeup. In the 1920s, the compelling Sufi-influenced teacher George I. Gurdjieff compared our ordinary state-of-being to a ship at sea. The ship's crew has mutinied, captured the captain, and left him tied up in the hold. Once they have locked him away, various crew members begin fighting one another for control of the wheel. One crew member overpowers the others, and temporarily steers the ship in one direction. Then he is overpowered by a second crew member, who steers in another direction, and so on. A ceaseless struggle rages for control of the ship, which goes one way, then another way, zigzagging constantly. Only by sheer luck does the ship manage to stay afloat at all. If the ship has any chance of arriving safely in port, the crew must reunite, reestablishing the captain at the helm, and let him steer the ship.

Of course, the embattled ship represents our everyday mind, and the crew members our constantly changing flow of images, thoughts, and desires. They flit here and there endlessly, completely undisciplined. Only when we place a disciplined captain decisively in charge of the whole mind-crew—which is precisely what meditation is designed to accomplish—do we have a reasonable chance of sailing our inner ship safely and harmoniously through the straits of life.

## Problems in Meditating

Meditation definitely causes problems. The simplest of these I like to call "distractions": minor bodily itches and cramps, mind wandering, and daydreaming. Whatever form of meditation you practice, even though your intent is the best, you will find that your mind wanders or that you start to daydream. One time or another, you will be sitting there and realize suddenly, "I've been daydreaming for all this time!"

Then, you will attempt to bring your focus back to your breathing or to your visualization. But after a brief period of concentration, you will be daydreaming again.

Now, such distractions are relatively insignificant. They happen to everybody who tries meditation, and there is an effective way to deal with them. As I said earlier, the itching and the cramps indicate that your physical giant is trying to prevent itself from being put to sleep. As for the mental distractions, whenever your mind starts to wander, it is useful to bear in mind the following analogy.

Imagine a loving mother who is taking her preschool child somewhere. They must arrive by a certain time. As they are walking, the child sees a flower and runs to smell its fragrance. The mother feels she is somewhat in a bind. Although they do not have much time for strolling, she is unwilling to yank her child away from this beautiful way of relating to nature. The mother must find a way through love and gentleness to coax the child away from the flower, without making the child feel ashamed or guilty. Perhaps the mother will say, "When we come back from our appointment, you can spend more time with this flower. But now we have to go." And with that the mother leads her child gently back to the path.

Then the child sees a brightly colored ribbon on the ground and runs over to pick it up. Her mother calls out, "Come back. You can see the ribbon later!" Next, the child notices a stray kitten and dashes over to pet it. Again the mother must bring the child back to the path. As anyone familiar with children knows, a walk with a child may be filled with many such moments. No matter how many times the mother brings the child back, the child will be ready to run off at the very next distraction.

Think about this situation for a moment. Is the child being mean, malicious, or disrespectful? Absolutely not, because as far as the child is concerned, the time pressure felt by her mother has neither personal meaning nor relevance. Go and tell a three year old that it's four-thirty, and you have to be somewhere at five o'clock! The words have literally no meaning; they might as well be nonsense syllables. A child of that age lacks completely an adult conception of time. So the adult must be patient with the child if their walk together is to be enjoyable at all.

In a sense, we are somewhat reversing the order with this analogy. When you sit down to meditate, your mind will resemble the child, running off in various directions. For instance, you will say, "I'm going to focus my attention on this particular meditative symbol." But after a few minutes or even sooner, you will discover that you are no longer focused on the image, but are thinking instead about other matters.

When you lose your focus, your conscious mind is like the child running off to play with something. Then, when you bring it back to the task, it will run off to play again, and you will once more have to bring it back. No matter what you do, the process of meditation will necessitate this routine over and over again. How many times? A hundred thousand times.

Do not believe that the essence of meditation is to sit without the mind wandering. Rather, meditation is precisely this challenging process of bringing the mind constantly back to its focus.

## OVERCOMING THE BARRIER

The next negative aspect of meditation is what I call "the barrier." This barrier can be physical or mental, and it is quite different from a distraction. The barrier is something that will not let us pass, like a roadblock which prevents our automobile from moving along the highway.

I can offer a vivid example from my own experience. When I was first learning sitting meditation, I began to meditate for increasing periods of time: first, five minutes, then ten minutes, then fifteen minutes. To my delight, I was able to meditate for a longer period than anyone in my class. I was becoming a bit arrogant from this awareness.

One day, therefore, I decided to set my timer for twenty minutes. After about eighteen minutes, however, I experienced an excruciating pain in my left knee. It was perhaps the worst physical pain of my life. I thought immediately that something horrible had happened to my knee. I jumped up from my meditative state to examine it, but lo and behold, my knee was fine. As soon as I stopped meditating and opened my eyes, the pain disappeared. I moved my knee. I walked. I could not believe it.

Despite my knowledge as a physician, I simply did not know what had happened. The next day, I again set my timer for twenty minutes, but at eighteen minutes I experienced the same pain in my knee. Though I began to suspect a mental connection, it took me another day or two to really accept that the excruciating pain in my knee would end the instant that I stopped meditating.

I decided that I would go ahead with my meditation anyway. I reasoned that two minutes of pain was hardly an eternity. For the next three months, I kept trying to make it to twenty minutes, but I never succeeded. No matter how much I psyched myself up to attain my objective and no matter how much I increased my tolerance for physical pain, it was as though someone always kept shifting the dial one notch past my limit.

I offer this account with the hope that you will not repeat my mistake. A barrier to meditation can be physical or mental; it can manifest itself as pain or as heightened anxiety. Unfortunately, few books on meditation mention this problem, but let me assure you that it is both real and common. Despite your good intentions, you can nevertheless find your inner development halted by a barrier. Perhaps, mental barriers are worse than physical ones, because they can make you quite anxious. I guarantee that if you hit a mental barrier, you will become aware of it very quickly. But the positive feature about barriers is that the pain or anxiety will vanish the moment you stop your meditative session. Nothing will bother you later in the day or evening: there will be no lingering effect. You will experience the barrier only when you are actually meditating.

Now, these blockages are quite individualized. They can manifest at any time during meditative practice. Yet, in an important way, a barrier is actually a good friend. It resembles a warning sign, like a roadblock that cautions you that the bridge ahead is washed out—or, a sign that warns that the road contains a large pothole, and that if you keep driving, you will hit it and possibly overturn.

In other words, somebody has been kind enough to say, "Stop here!" If you understand this concept, you will not fight the barrier. Rather, you will respect it and know that it is there to protect you, not hurt you.

In practical terms, then, how should we deal with the barrier? First, recognize it as an ally. Eventually, whenever my knee hurt during meditation, I would say, "Okay, thank you," and end the session. I no longer felt frustrated or that I was struggling. Then one day, I set my timer for twenty minutes, and reached my goal at last! The timer rang, yet I felt absolutely no pain.

This whole episode took place several years ago, and I have never felt that knee pain again. Why? Because it had served its purpose. I had been proceeding too quickly in my practice, and I needed something to slow me down. And so, a part of me—physical, mental, or spiritual—was kind enough to warn me. After months of painful struggle, I understood that something within me had matured or developed sufficiently so that I could go forward.

I have seen what can happen to people who refuse to slow down but try instead to crash through their barriers. I am now grateful that I had one. Of course, if you proceed slowly enough with meditation, you may never encounter a barrier. But regardless of whether you reach a barrier or not, you should know that there are processes in nature that require the passage of time. An old Native American adage says, "You can't make corn grow faster by pulling up on the stalks."

If we try nevertheless, we might destroy the entire plant. Suppose we are feeling impatient about the growth of a tiny seed in our garden. Would it make any sense to break open the plant with a screwdriver to make the seed sprout faster? Of course not. We would kill the living thing. We cannot rush nature. The seed must lie dormant in the soil for a certain period of time before it sprouts and takes root as a plant. However benevolent we may feel about our garden, we do not use a screwdriver to make the seeds grow faster.

An analogous, spiritual maturational process takes place inside us, and it likewise needs a definite amount of time. Every living thing has a particular gestation period, and birth cannot be hurried. We know that premature births are risky and carry no benefits. Therefore, we should seek "full-term growth" to best enhance our self-worth through meditative practice.

It is often difficult for us to accept the idea that growth is occurring when we see nothing happening outwardly. Yet, we know that when we plant a seed in fertile soil, development must be taking place. Somehow, we can accept this notion more easily about our garden plants than about ourselves.

It is hard to believe that we are growing each time we meditate, when the changes within us are not readily apparent. But this is precisely where the issue of discipline is most relevant. Only later can we actually see clear changes in our personality and behavior—similar to a plant's buds coming forth. Before this blossoming occurs, we must trust that growth is underway though we cannot observe it with our senses.

## Dangers on the Path

So far, we have discussed distractions and barriers. Now we come to dangers. How can there be dangers associated with something as beneficial to us as meditation? Haven't I emphasized how helpful meditation is for enhancing our self-worth? However, no force in the universe can be wholly good and lack the potential for evil. Power always has both good and evil possibilities. If meditation is a powerful tool, then it can certainly be misused.

A danger is different from a barrier, because a barrier ceases to manifest the moment we stop meditating. By contrast, a danger may not even occur while we are engaged in meditation, but instead will be coincidental with our meditation. That is, we may find ourselves having frequent nightmares. Or, we may experience severe headaches for the first time in our life. Or, we may have intense anxiety attacks during the day, or develop sharp pains in our joints. Sometimes, such discomforts occur when we are actually meditating, and sometimes not. But when we stop meditating for a few days, these discomforts typically vanish. Unfortunately, when we resume meditation, these discomforts or pains often arise again.

Dealing with dangers is definitely more troublesome than dealing with barriers. I have known people who have reported headaches, insomnia, restlessness, sensory changes, even hallucinations. These hallucinations do not always occur while the person is meditating, but at other times of the day or night. Other individuals report memory loss, or paranoid or disassociative states in which they are actually awake but everything seems dreamlike and unreal. These moods can come on suddenly—a person may be chatting in a room with others, and then in an instant, everything takes on a distant, unreal quality. Because one is awake, mental states like these involving ego loss can be truly frightening.

If we persist in meditating despite these occurrences, they can develop a life of their own. That is, weeks after we have stopped our meditation, we may still experience nightmares, intense anxiety, persistent physical pains, or disassociative states. As a practicing psychiatrist, I have found that psychiatric hospitals house a small percentage of patients suffering from these sorts of phenomena. Such dangerous symptoms can result not only from meditation, but from other causes as well. The issue is that there are many inner forces and energies about which psychiatry knows very little. We are ordinarily shielded from such phenomena by our own ignorance, but when we begin to remove some of the shielding and explore unknown regions within, we become more vulnerable to these dangers.

For this reason, our rules for meditation are really necessary precautions. They help us steer clear of the dangers, whereas disobeying the rules makes us more susceptible to them. I can illustrate this concept clearly through an analogy to learning to drive a car. If you have never driven before, I could warn you about one danger after another. I could tell you about the possibility of horrible automobile accidents. I could get slides of head-on collisions and show you graphically the dangers of driving. However, like most people, you probably fully comprehend these risks already. We are all aware of how many people are killed or maimed each year, and yet we all drive anyway.

Why? Because there is clearly much benefit to driving, and life would be very different if we refused to drive because of the dangers. The benefits of driving clearly outweigh the risks. We know that if we obey the traffic rules—even though they do not always make sense—we will have a much better chance of avoiding the dangers than if we ignore the rules.

There are dangers to meditating, just as there are dangers to driving a car. It is not my intent to overplay these dangers, but be aware that they do exist. It would be unethical for a driving instructor to put you in the driver's seat and say, "Don't worry about anything. Just turn on the ignition and do whatever feels best." This approach would be irresponsible and would increase your chances of getting hurt. The more cognizant you are of the dangers in driving a car, the safer you will be. The same principle holds true for meditation.

Centering and grounding are so important because if we are well-rooted like a tree, then we can go "out on a limb" safely. Or, to use another metaphor, though we may be able to reach the fiftieth or hundredth floor of a skyscraper, we need to have a way of getting back to the ground floor. Reaching higher inner states is one matter. Returning is another. We should never seek to attain realms from which the way back to ordinary consciousness is unclear.

In my psychiatric practice, I have seen many young people in hospitals in exactly this situation. They are stuck somewhere on another "floor" of consciousness, and are unable to return to everyday reality. They may be labeled as schizophrenic or psychotic, and treated with psychotropic drugs, but what they really need is help bringing their "elevator" back to the ground floor.

So when you meditate and something unfamiliar starts to happen, make sure to discuss the matter with a reliable teacher. If there is nobody to ask, and you experience persistent mental or physical discomfort, it is a good idea to stop meditating. As an absolute minimum, stop for at least a month. The discomforts may be telling you that you need to be more grounded. You may need to take a course in *T'ai Chi*, or some other time-honored method of centering. In Chapter 7, I discuss a variety of such approaches.

How likely are people to experience harmful effects from meditating? Not very likely, for two key reasons. First, most meditators are performing only deep relaxation exercises, and rarely get past the "ground floor" anyway. Those who do engage in serious meditative practice tend to join a religious community, where they are guided by knowledgeable teachers, and their meditation is integrated into an ongoing and cumulative lifestyle. Such persons are not likely to experience dangers.

However, the real at risk group for meditation generally includes the small group of people who attempt advanced meditation after reading a book or hearing a little about it. Even more foolhardy are those who combine meditation with drugs. What happens then is that the drug opens the body's energy centers and magnifies the dangers of meditating in people who are not adequately grounded first.

In short, meditation is a powerful tool affecting our consciousness. Like all tools, it should be treated with respect and utilized properly. If we follow these basic guidelines and proceed slowly and methodically, we will find meditation a wonderful means for enhancing our self-worth, benefiting all aspects of our life. With this in mind, let us look at some specific meditation techniques.

# 6

# Techniques of Inner Peace

*Be still, and know that I am God.*
Psalm 46:10

This chapter provides practical instruction in a variety of meditative exercises. Deriving from time-honored spiritual traditions from around the world, each is an effective way to enhance self-worth. There is no single form of meditation that is intrinsically better than all the others. Each is capable of producing positive results. However, you may discover a specific method of meditation especially beneficial or intriguing. If so, you will profit by practicing it diligently.

The number of different types of meditation is potentially infinite. We can transform virtually any activity into a meditative exercise by becoming absorbed in it to the exclusion of other thoughts, feelings, and actions. Hence, it is legitimate to create your own meditations out of seemingly mundane activities, such as washing dishes, showering, or shaving. Beginners usually feel the need for firmer structure, though, and are consequently most comfortable practicing established meditations.

You will generally find it easier to meditate, or even do preliminary relaxation, if you listen to the directions instead of reading them. You might wish to make a cassette recording in your own voice of this entire chapter. Speak into the microphone as though you were guiding someone else through each technique. Then you can play the recording whenever you wish to meditate or relax.

As I mentioned earlier, it is vital that you stay awake when you are meditating. I therefore recommend that you sit comfortably with your spine erect. Do not lie down. However, because the relaxation exercises have a different function, you may perform them while lying in bed, and allow them to gently lead into soothing sleep.

## PRELIMINARY RELAXATION EXERCISES

### *Exercise #1.* Muscle Relaxation

This exercise is a variant of a method called progressive relaxation. It is based on the idea that how relaxed our muscles are is related to how relaxed we feel emotionally. This is hardly a radical concept; popular language demonstrates an awareness of this vital link. For example, when a person is tense, we say that he or she is "uptight." This comment accurately describes the tightening up of that person's muscles.

The more muscles you relax, the more relaxed you will feel. The deeper you relax your muscles, the deeper your sense of relaxation will be.

While doing this exercise, some people experience a

feeling of lightness, almost as though their bodies were floating. Others describe a feeling of heaviness, as if their bodies were weighed down with lead. Still others feel a pleasant warm or tingling sensation in their limbs.

These are all typical reactions to muscle relaxation and generally no cause for worry. Indeed, they often enhance the process of relaxation and make it more pleasurable. However, if you find these sensations disquieting or bothersome, it is best to stop this exercise and seek advice from someone knowledgeable before proceeding. Of course, it is possible to relax deeply without experiencing any such sensations.

Now to begin. Close your eyes and focus your awareness on your feet. Picture them clearly in your mind's eye, and be aware of any tension. If you are unable to sense these muscles, or others mentioned later in this exercise, you can purposely tense them momentarily and keep them as tight as you can. When you release the tension, you can more easily discern the difference between a muscle's "tight" and "loose" conditions.

When your feet have relaxed, shift your awareness to both legs up to the knees, and relax these muscles. Then, let the relaxation spread into your thighs. Bring your awareness next to relaxing your pelvis and buttocks; then relax your buttocks and lower back.

Now, focus on your chest. Your breathing can help to relax your chest muscles and also deepen the sense of relaxation growing throughout your body. Each time you breathe out, feel your chest sink in. As your chest contracts, imagine that your whole body is sinking into a pleasant, comfortable, and relaxed state.

With each out-breath allow yourself to go deeper and deeper into the relaxation. From this point on in the exercise, relax more and more of your body with each out-breath, no matter which body part you are focusing on at the moment. For example, after relaxing your chest, bring your awareness to your back and increase the looseness in these muscles. While doing this, continue to deepen your overall relaxation with each exhalation.

Next, allow your shoulder muscles to relax, and from the shoulders let the relaxation spread down into both arms. Then, relax both forearms. Following this, relax your hands all the way to your fingertips. Then, relax your neck by allowing the neck muscles to loosen so that they no longer hold up your head. From the neck, let the relaxation spread up the back of your head and through your scalp.

Then, let the relaxed feeling flow into your forehead and from there into your eyes. Like breathing, relaxing the eyes is a key aspect of deepening your overall sense of relaxation. After your eyes are relaxed, relax other portions of your face, your cheeks, nose, lips, mouth, tongue, throat, jaws, and chin.

After completing this circuit of your body, do a brief scan to see if any parts need additional help. If so, you can relax a particular section of your body directly, or indirectly, by working on your breathing.

Some people prefer to perform this exercise starting with their heads and working their way down to their feet. The order is a matter of personal preference. Each gives comparable results.

## *Exercise #2.* Relaxation through Warmth Awareness

This exercise is similar to the first, but it focuses on a sense of warmth or heat instead of muscle relaxation. It too has been practiced for centuries. In this regard, it is striking to note a parallel to biofeedback: the two most successful relaxation modalities are the EMG feedback machines that aid in muscle relaxation and the temperature feedback machines that aid in elevating skin temperature.

To perform this exercise, sit comfortably with your eyes closed. Choose a spot on your head or forehead, and make this spot feel warm. You can accomplish this by imagining that the sun is shining brightly, with its rays striking your head on that spot. Or you can imagine that you are sending extra blood, and with it heat, to this part of your body.

Once you begin to warm the spot, spread the warmth over your entire head. When your head becomes warm, spread the warmth over your face, and then over your neck. Continue to spread this sensation of heat down your torso and limbs, until your entire body from head to feet is suffused by warmth. As warmth envelops you, so will a growing sense of relaxation. The warmer you can make yourself, the deeper will be your accompanying relaxation.

Here again, the order can be reversed—feet to head rather than head to feet. Although this exercise can be very potent, it takes patience to experience a sense of warmth, and more patience before this sensation can be maintained and spread throughout your body.

## BREATHING MEDITATIONS

Down through the centuries, many kinds of meditation have been developed that focus on the breath. In one form or another, breathing meditations have long been practiced by people all over the globe.

### *Exercise* #3. Breath Counting

Sit comfortably with your eyes closed. Focus your awareness on your breathing. Each time you exhale, silently count a number. Start with "one" for the first exhalation; then count "two" for the second, "three" for the third, and "four" for the fourth. "Four" is as high as you should go.

On the fifth exhalation, start with "one" again and continue until you reach "four." At that point, return again to "one." Continue in this manner for the duration of the meditation.

There is nothing special about counting up to four. If, for some reason, you prefer another number such as seven, you can count up to seven and continue to use cycles of seven. The number you choose is not particularly important, but it is advisable that it be less than 10.

Why? Because having to count to a large number can be confusing, and it places an extra burden on your concentration. Counting to a high number can also tempt you into keeping score: "Last time I got up to 219. Let's see if I can beat that record today. Bob is up to 305, so I want to reach at least number—."

During this meditation, thinking about anything other than your breathing and the number you have assigned to each exhalation is a distraction. Ignore it!

## *Exercise #4.* Rhythmic Breathing

Many spiritual traditions have taught that our rate of breathing sets up a vibratory frequency that influences our entire body. When this frequency is synchronized with a natural rhythm such as heartbeat, it has a unifying effect on us. As a prerequisite for more advanced meditations, such traditions often teach rhythmic breathing based on heartbeat.

This breathing exercise can be used as a meditation in and of itself, or as a method of breathing while you are doing a meditation that is not focused on the breath. In this exercise, your breathing rhythm is set by your heartbeat.

Sit comfortably, preferably with your eyes closed. Place your finger on your pulse so that you can determine and keep track of your heartbeat. Before beginning this meditation, take in several short inhalations (without exhaling), one per heartbeat, until your lungs are full.

Determine the number of short in-breaths (or heartbeats) you need to make up a full inhalation. You may adjust your breathing if necessary, so that this comes to an even number. The specific number of short in-breaths is not important, so long as you are comfortable with it.

Suppose that you require six short in-breaths to complete your inhalation. The rhythm of breathing during the meditation will then have four parts: 1) inhale for six short breaths (one per heartbeat); 2) hold your breath for three heartbeats; 3) breathe out completely in six short out-breaths (one per heartbeat); and 4) hold your breath for three heartbeats. Then begin the cycle again.

During each cycle, the number of breaths on which you inhale should equal the number of breaths on which you exhale. The rate of your breathing is determined by the rate of your heart. There is a pause at the end of each complete inhalation and another pause at the end of each complete exhalation. You hold each of these pauses for a count half as long as the number of in-breaths or out-breaths. In other words, you hold your breath for half the total number of heartbeats in each full inhalation or exhalation.

Should your heart rate change during the meditation, you can adjust your breathing accordingly. However, you should maintain the same ratio of pause to inhalation and exhalation.

If your heart rate is steady and its rhythm clearly apparent, you can let go of your pulse but continue to follow its rhythm. Another alternative once you have measured your heartbeat and determined its steadiness is to use a metronome, setting it to the rate of your heart. Then, the rhythm of your breathing can follow the clicking of the metronome.

## HEIGHTENING AWARENESS

### *Exercise* #5. Visual Contemplation

Typically, we go through our days focused almost entirely on externals. At other times, though rarely by our volition, we become aware of cosmic unity. Psychologist Abraham Maslow called these rare occasions of awareness "peak experiences." This exercise helps to give us an awareness of the interconnection between the world of the one and the world of the many.

Stand very close to a painting. Select one spot on the picture—not an unusual or outstanding spot—and concentrate your attention on it. See the spot as a separate entity, a spot unto itself, that exists apart from the rest of the picture.

Next, keeping your gaze on the spot, slowly move back away from the painting until you reach a point where you can see the entire painting clearly and the single spot as a part of it. Then, continuing to stare at the spot, move forward again until it once more becomes a separate entity.

When you see the spot as isolated, it should be possible to cut away mentally the rest of the picture so that the spot continues to exist on its own. When you see the spot as an integral part of the picture, on the other hand, then the whole picture should seem to suffer if the spot is removed. This exercise will generally give better results if you focus on what is considered good artwork. The reason is that in fine art, each part of the picture is integrally related to the whole.

## *Exercise #6.* Verbalizing Awareness

In this meditation, you may keep your eyes open or closed, as you wish. Make up a series of sentences. Begin each sentence with the phrase, "I am aware of *blank*," and complete the sentence with whatever you happen to be perceiving at the moment. As soon as you finish each sentence, immediately formulate another one.

As you continue, you may notice that your awareness is mainly focused on things in your external environment, such as trees, birds, or cars. If this is the case, begin to pay more attention to what you are experiencing inside.

Conversely, if your awareness largely concerns your inner world of thoughts, feelings, or body sensations, then devote more attention to your environment.

If your mind becomes blank at any time, you might say, "I am aware of *my mind being blank.*" If this exercise seems silly, you might say, "I am aware *that doing this exercise makes me feel silly.*"

I recommend that you repeat this exercise often, for at least a few minutes. It does not require special sessions, for you can do it effectively while walking on the street or sitting in a bus or train.

Some people find this exercise extremely beneficial, because it helps them become more conscious of the here and now. To make even better use of this technique, pay particular attention to those times when your mind goes blank. When you find suddenly that your awareness has closed off, it is usually because you have started to become aware of something anxiety arousing, and your mind has shut down as a defensive or protective measure.

However, if you allow yourself to stay with the blankness and do nothing to disrupt it, your emptiness will spontaneously dissipate. Eventually, a previously suppressed image, thought, or feeling will pierce through into consciousness. This spontaneous material usually offers a clue about the other censored material.

## *Exercise* #7. Awareness of Eating

This exercise, centered on the act of eating, can be especially interesting. However, it needs to be performed when you have ample time to spend at the dinner table. You can practice it alone or with a group, but in either case, do not speak to anyone.

Begin by focusing visually for a couple of minutes on the plate of food in front of you. Then eat only one type of food from the plate at a time. For example, if you have a plate of fish, carrots, and potatoes, choose any one of the three for your first taste. The second taste can be a different food, but avoid putting two kinds of food in your mouth at the same time.

While the food is in your mouth, do not hold onto your knife, fork, or spoon. Put the utensils down on the table. Chew very, very slowly, and savor each taste. Wait until you have completely finished chewing, tasting, and swallowing whatever food you have in your mouth before taking another bite. Finish the meal in this manner.

It is possible to use this method in a similar fashion with your sense of smell, sound, or touch.

## *Exercise* #8. Double Awareness

Giving up self-contact in order to make contact with another can seem to be a form of self-betrayal. The purpose of this exercise, therefore, is to help you learn to be close to others without losing yourself in the process.

This exercise is best done with a partner. Sit close together, preferably on the floor, facing each other. Close your eyes and focus your attention on yourself. Make and maintain contact with some aspect of yourself. That is, become aware of something you are experiencing, either a physical sensation, a feeling, or an idea or image. At different times, you might experiment with all three.

Now, open your eyes and make contact with your partner. As you do so, note carefully what happens to your self-contact. Most people either lose their self-awareness or experience its diminution when they become conscious of something else.

As soon as your self-contact starts to diminish, immediately close your eyes and reestablish the contact. When you are again aware of yourself, open your eyes and reestablish contact with your partner. You should maintain contact only as long as your self-contact remains strong.

Practice this exercise by repeating the cycle: first, closing your eyes to establish self-contact, and then opening your eyes and relating to your partner only when you can hold on to self-contact.

If you feel overwhelmed while performing this exercise with a partner, you can start by working with an inanimate object or a simple living thing like a plant. When you can do this comfortably, then try the exercise with a friend.

When you perform this exercise with another person, your partner can initially remain passive. Later, the two of you can switch roles, or you can perform the exercise simultaneously. When you practice simultaneous awareness, there will be times when you open your eyes and find that your partner's eyes are closed; close after yours; are open; or open after yours open. You may find that you react differently in each of these situations. You should practice this exercise until you are comfortable with each of its four phases.

## MEDITATIONS FOR THE MENTALLY RESTLESS

Some meditations actually take advantage of the many thoughts that come into our awareness when we try to quiet our minds. Such techniques cleverly use thoughts as the focus of the meditation, and therefore often appeal to those who are intellectually oriented. The next two exercises illustrate this approach.

### *Exercise #9.* Balloon/Bubble Meditation

Sit comfortably with your eyes closed. As the first thought comes into your mind, use your imagination to place the thought inside a helium-filled balloon—or, if you prefer, inside a translucent bubble or puff of smoke. In your mind's eye, watch the balloon rise until it ascends beyond your field of vision; this usually takes two to five seconds. As your next thought arises, place it inside another balloon and send it aloft. Continue to send up thought-balloons until the timer indicates that your meditation session is over.

The thought that you should put into the balloon is the one foremost in your mind at the moment the balloon is launched. It can be an idea, image, memory, or feeling. Should another thought arise while you are watching the last balloon, you can acknowledge that thought (which we can call thought #2), and tell it that it has to wait its turn.

When the balloon you are watching has floated beyond your field of vision, then create a balloon for

thought #2. However, if another thought (thought #3) becomes foremost even though thought #2 has been waiting, then put thought #3 in the next balloon.

Sometimes, the same thought will recur over and over. If this happens, just send it aloft each time in a separate balloon. On occasion, a single thought, for example one about a family member, triggers a series of similar thoughts, and one family member after another comes to mind. If this occurs, send each thought skyward in its own balloon. If a thought is about a group of people, then the whole group can all go into one balloon.

Ironically, it is not unusual when you perform this meditation to experience extended periods of time in which no thoughts come to mind at all. You can handle this by waiting for new thoughts, but it is usually easier to send up empty balloons.

The balloons, bubbles, or puffs of smoke serve as

both timing devices and separation devices, isolating thoughts from one another and giving each a certain amount of your time. When you practice this exercise, it is important that you do not become involved in analyzing the connections between your thoughts. Although you can learn much from such analysis, the time for scrutiny is after, not during, the meditation.

## *Exercise #10.*
## One Thousand-Petaled Lotus Meditation

This exercise is based on the concept that each object in the cosmos is vitally linked to everything else. In Eastern tradition, the lotus is a symbol whose petals represent the endless connections among all forms of life. The number "one thousand" stands for infinity.

Sit comfortably with your eyes closed. Before starting this meditation, choose a word to serve as a central concept about which you will form mental associations, for example, "light."

Begin by focusing on the word and then wait for your first association. Suppose it is "sun." Think about

the link between "light" and "sun" for three to four seconds. It is not important whether you see the connection between the two thoughts.

When three to four seconds have elapsed, focus again on "light" and wait for the next thought to arise, perhaps, "dark." Examine the connection between these two words for the next few seconds. Then return again to "light."

However, suppose your next thought is "elephant." You see no connection between "light" and "elephant." After thinking about this lack of connection for several seconds, go back to "light" anyway.

Continue this process for the length of the meditation session, until your timer rings. The same associations, such as "light" and "sun," may repeat themselves. That is all right. You can, but need not, use a different word each time that you do this meditation.

## MANTRA (SOUND) MEDITATIONS

The next type of meditation uses a mantra. In this system, a word, sound, phrase, or series of phrases or sounds is chanted over and over. Some mantras are spoken aloud and others repeated silently. Of all the kinds of meditation practiced in the West today, mantra meditations have been among the most popular. For example, Transcendental Meditation (TM), which has been widely practiced in North America and Western Europe, uses a type of mantra. Mantra meditation lends itself to being practiced in a group, in which all chant the same mantra aloud in unison.

Religious prayer is often a form of mantra meditation. Prayers incorporate phrases that are repeated in devotion either alone or in a group. Many prayers that have become basic to major religions were originally composed by charismatic leaders as their personal mantras. When these individuals came to be revered as holy, and particularly when they were believed to possess extraordinary powers, it was common practice for their followers to adopt such mantras in adoration. In time, these mantras were collected into prayerbooks.

However, such prayers usually possess little power unless they are recited with the dedication and mental discipline of their composers. Consequently, many people who use religious prayerbooks today are unaware of the origin of various prayers as forms of mantra meditation.

## *Exercise #11.* Mantra Meditation

Sit comfortably with your eyes closed. Choose any sound or phrase that is pleasing or holds special significance for you. It is not important that you fully understand its meaning. Some people prefer to use a traditional spiritual symbol such as a name of God, for example, the Hebrew word "Eh-Lo-Him" from the Bible or the Sanskrit "Om." Others prefer a neutral word such as "one"; still others, a poetic phrase.

Does it matter which mantra you select? As discussed in Chapter 4, the world's great religions all hold that it does. Different mantras exert different effects on us. But if your chief purpose is to strengthen your self-worth, virtually any word without negative associations will be beneficial for you.

Begin saying your mantra aloud or silently, and repeat it over and over until the timer rings and your meditation ends.

You may also wish to follow a progressive pattern in this meditation, though it is not absolutely necessary. The pattern has three steps. The first step is to say the mantra aloud while meditating. You can practice it too at other times of the day when you have a few spare minutes. Step two consists of saying the mantra silently to yourself, without moving your lips. This too can be performed at various times of the day.

Step three consists of being able to hear the mantra inside yourself without either saying it aloud or repeating it silently. If you practice steps one and two long enough, the mantra's sound can become so familiar that it seems like a tape recording that you can hear at will. Then, even when you are engaged in other activities—and particularly during times of stress—you can turn the mantra on as a kind of background music.

Hearing the mantra in this way will generally not interfere with what you are doing. Rather, it can bring with it the sense of relaxation, peace, and calmness that accompanies meditation. Similarly, you can mentally "play" your mantra when you are involved in a protracted routine or boring activity. At these moments, you can listen to your mantra, and not only be relaxed, but also find that time passes quickly, without your being so aware of it.

Richard Alpert (Ram Dass), teacher of meditation, has commented that when your mantra becomes internalized as in step three, "instead of your doing the mantra, the mantra is doing you." Such a state is a worthwhile goal and one that can definitely help strengthen self-worth.

Remember our tale of the man in Chapter 3 who poured water onto the ground? In like manner, a sturdy and towering tree will eventually emerge from your inner ground. But it will not happen overnight, and daily watering is necessary for healthy and vibrant growth. Meditation is one simple daily practice that can help. Becoming aware of our body and its life energy flow is another way to facilitate inner growth. It is to this intriguing subject that we now turn.

# 7

# Choreography of Mind and Body: The Martial Arts

*Nothing under heaven is softer or more yielding than water. But when it attacks things hard and resistant, there is not one of them that can prevail. The principle that the yielding conquers the resistant and soft conquers hard is a fact known to all, yet few persons utilize it properly.*

Lao Tzu

When we lose touch with core elements of our being, we forfeit much of our sense of self-worth and are left with feelings of inner loss and emptiness. By seeking fulfillment in things that satisfy only our physical senses or our superficial mental interests, we achieve at best a temporary respite from the gnawing void within us. Yet, this same void is actually occupied by an inner energy that both allows us to thrive, and connects us to the spiritual. The gnawing is its call to us, its cry for our attention. This life force demands our recognition. If we deny it, we feel less than whole and ultimately deny our self-worth.

Harmony of body, mind, and spirit is a central goal of the internally focused systems of Asian martial arts. These time-honored disciplines are based on the concept of an internal life force which links us with everything else. They further teach that each of us can become aware of this vital energy and learn to channel it in constructive ways. Thus, many Eastern martial arts are eminently practical "water-pouring" exercises, exquisitely effective in fostering self-worth.

In the United States, the martial arts are largely thought of as methods of self-defense or as athletic skills for competing in hand-to-hand combat. Yet, fighting characterizes the various Asian martial arts no more than celibacy characterizes the priesthood. That is, particularly as the term "martial" relates to the internal aspects of these disciplines, fighting is a minor and relatively insignificant part of an entire way of life. If we examine the *non*-martial elements of the martial arts, we can begin to appreciate their relationship to self-worth. Intrigued by the pragmatic application of Eastern fighting techniques, however, Americans have all too eagerly lifted the martial arts out of their original cultural and religious contexts and erroneously interpreted them as systems of combat whole onto themselves. The presence in most American cities of storefront schools offering to teach Asian fighting techniques to anyone with ready cash speaks to my point.

Physical combat is probably as old as humanity, and the martial arts did originate as fighting skills. Indeed, they undoubtedly served as means of both self-defense and attack. Although martial arts seem to have been most fully developed in Asia, some aspects of Asian combat had a Western counterpart two thousand years ago. For example, Plato mentioned the discipline of *skiamachia*—combat without an antagonist—an ancient form of shadow boxing. Moreover, as ancient literature, art, and sculpture demonstrate, wrestling has been extolled in India as a sport and means of exercise since 1500 B.C. To this day, it remains a popular sport there.

In China, the fighting arts can be traced back thousands of years. As combative techniques, the early forms of Chinese wrestling were rather primitive. For instance, farmers often wrestled by placing cow horns over their heads and attempting to butt one another. Eventually, such fighting methods grew in popularity and sophistication and came under the influence of the emerging discipline called Taoism. Thus were born the "internal" systems of martial arts.

The martial arts utilize techniques that can be broadly categorized as either external or internal. Today, many systems integrate both components. In general, the external systems favor muscular exercise and stress the use of fists and feet as weapons. They focus primarily on the art of hand-to-hand combat. In contrast, the internal systems deemphasize aggression and emphasize softness, will, and mental strength instead. They also promote healthful relaxation through exercise and teach as well an alternative way of living.

The origins of the internal martial arts can be traced to early Taoist writings such as the *Tao Te Ching* by Lao Tzu. Born about 570 B.C., Lao Tzu was an iconoclastic sage and mystic who rejected the common violent practices of his time such as horn-butting. He insisted that the qualities of softness and pliability should be the hallmarks of healthy individual existence. His successor, Chuang Tzu, promulgated the same outlook and emphasized the importance of proper breathing for daily health:

> You must concentrate and not listen with your eyes, but with your heart. Then, without listening with the heart, do so with breath. The ear is limited to ordinary listening, the heart to the rational. Listening with the breath, one awaits things uncommittedly.

Mencius, a contemporary of Chuang Tzu, added to these internal exercises by stressing the will and acknowledging the flow of *chi*—vital energy or life energy. "If the will is concentrated," Mencius observed, "the vital energy will follow it and become active. . . . Will is of the highest importance." Mencius believed that the power of the will and chi could be cultivated only through righteous living and good deeds.

Other Taoist doctrines taught that people should refrain from actions which are contrary to nature—that is, they should absorb attacks effortlessly and respond to events spontaneously. These doctrines were also foundation stones of the internal systems of martial arts. Principles of meditation and relaxation were incorporated into these systems, as were rules about hygiene and health maintenance. Taoist ideas were applied to many aspects of everyday living, including diet and nutrition, the use of herbs, and the practice of exercises to strengthen our mind and hormonal system.

The internal systems of martial arts refined and retained those fighting skills that depended on internal energy—chi—rather than on brute physical strength. They stressed that one triumphs in battle by being like water, which is soft and subtly yielding yet can overcome substances which are hard and inflexible. Fighting skills were taught chiefly as a means of self-defense. A master would engage in physical combat only as a last resort, and even then would do so only with extreme reluctance and restraint.

Thus, the internal approach to martial arts evolved slowly over the centuries into a way of life that was philosophically opposed to violence and dedicated to restoring all things on earth to their original harmony. Much of the accumulated knowledge of these traditions remains, taught in the form of exercises erroneously understood by most Westerners as mere combative techniques.

Unfortunately, it is possible to learn a martial art solely for its aggressive skills, such as how and where to strike an opponent during street fighting. However, this superficial approach applies only to the external aspects of the martial arts. We cannot master the internal systems without addressing ourselves first to serious study of the total and balanced lifestyle they embrace.

## CHI: THE UNIVERSAL LIFE ENERGY

The internal or soft forms of the martial arts are best exemplified by the ancient Chinese system known as T'ai Chi, which is currently gaining worldwide popularity. The name T'ai Chi means the "supreme ultimate" form of exercise, and it has been taught for centuries as a series of movements based on the concept of chi. One theory as to the origin of T'ai Chi is that Chang Son-feng, a Taoist sage living during the Yuan dynasty (1279-1368), learned it in a dream. However, most scholars acknowledge that the origins of this remarkable system are lost in the mists of antiquity.

It is not easy to grasp the essence of an art that lies far from mainstream Western beliefs, but a Zen parable may suggest a helpful approach to an alien body of knowledge such as T'ai Chi. In this story, a famous professor visits a humble Zen master to see what, if anything, he can learn. The two begin to converse, and the professor tries to make clear how learned he is in a multitude of academic disciplines. Finally, the Zen master offers some tea. The professor accepts, and his host begins pouring the tea. Soon the professor's little cup is full, yet the Zen master continues pouring. At first, the professor observes this odd behavior quietly, but as the tea spills over the sides of the cup and onto the floor, he cries out: "Why don't you stop pouring? Can't you see that the cup is full and that you are just wasting the tea?"

With a smile, the Zen master replies: "This is exactly what is happening with you. You have come to me with your cup already overflowing with knowledge, and I can therefore add nothing. To learn more, you must first be willing to empty your cup."

It is precisely such openness and receptivity, a willingness to let go of beliefs fixed by past experience, that will best enable us to appreciate the concept of chi and its relationship to the practice of T'ai Chi.

The concept of a subtle life force has been a familiar idea for centuries. Many philosophic systems postulate an underlying energy but do not see it in exactly the same light. Though the name of this energy varies according to the particular culture and historical period, there has been remarkable consensus among highly diverse traditions about the nature of this force.

In the Jewish Kabbalistic tradition, for example, this force is known as *ruach.* Ruach is said to underlie inner vitality, and it disappears at death. Esoteric Jewish teachings hold that ruach may be influenced by special body postures and breathing techniques. Although little has been written about subtle life energy in Native American cultures, oral sources suggest that it is a part of all living things and that a medicine man or woman can transfer it to help restore health to the sick. Islamic mystics, called Sufis, speak of a subtle force, called *baraka,* that can be transmitted from teacher to disciple to cause subtle changes in consciousness. The Sufis also believe that there are seven centers of *latifa* (bioenergy) in the body that influence mental and physical conditions.

Perhaps the most widely known Asian traditions that focus on the life energy are the Indian and Chinese systems of thought. According to ancient Sanskrit tradition, seven energy centers, or *chakras*, exist in the human body. They are located along the spine, and each, when awakened through specific methods, governs and stimulates particular physical, emotional, and spiritual functions. Each chakra is said to have a characteristic color, which appears as a ring or aura of light when observed through nonordinary perception. Furthermore, each chakra is believed to be affected in turn by special colors or sounds.

In Western medicine, we regard the human body as being made up of a number of interrelated systems, such as the cardiovascular, digestive, excretory, and reproductive systems. Eastern medicine accepts these but works on the basis of an additional system as well, based on chi. Chi is an omnipresent form of energy that permeates but is not limited to all matter. It is the basic energy from which all other known energies derive. Living organisms are said to have a greater concentration of chi than inanimate forms. Indeed, life depends on the ongoing circulation of this energy throughout the organism, in the same way life depends on the circulation of blood.

In traditional Chinese thought, the human body is seen as a complex network of subtle energies that influence our daily health and vitality. Just as blood circulates in set channels that we call arteries and veins, so does chi circulate in twelve set pathways called meridians. Ten of these meridians correspond to organs and two are concerned with the regulation of the entire body rather than with any particular organ. Each meridian has specific points that accurately reflect the health of a particular organ or body system. Disease is viewed as an external manifestation of an imbalance in this energy system. Each organ is thought to be closely related to overall physical vitality as well as to specific emotions. It is believed that long before disease becomes apparent, the meridian system will show the underlying disharmony, signaling that preventive healing should be initiated.

Thus, illness is regarded as originating in an imbalance in the flow of chi. For example, there may be too much or too little energy in any part of the organism, or an inappropriate amount within the organism in relation to its surroundings. Balance rather than the absolute quantity of chi is viewed as crucial. If an imbalance in chi is allowed to persist, it will eventually weaken the functioning of our physical body and in so doing give rise to physical or mental symptoms of distress. We can restore health by correcting the imbalance in life energy flow, either before or after overt physical symptoms become manifest, provided that irreversable physical damage has not yet occurred.

In traditional Chinese healing, various methods are used to diagnose the functional condition of the meridians. Some practitioners rely on the sense of touch and measure pulses at points throughout the body. Other healers make slow hand movements over the body and "feel" irregularities in the flow of chi. The goal of acupuncture and related methods of treatment is to restore the natural harmony of the chi network. Through applying pressure, heat, needles, electricity, ultrasound, or magnetism to specific points along the meridians, the healer carefully reestablishes a smooth, regular flow of energy throughout the body. Some illnesses are seen as manifestations of too much energy flow in particular organs, while others indicate inadequate amounts of the life force in certain organs or systems.

Current electromagnetic studies are providing scientific evidence for the existence of chi meridians. The evidence indicates that the meridians and their points are located precisely as described in centuries-old Oriental medical texts. Preventive medicine in the Chinese system means that people regularly take steps to maintain a balanced flow of chi. Such a regimen typically includes daily exercises like T'ai Chi.

## T'ai Chi: The Supreme System

The T'ai Chi exercise is composed of a series of flowing, graceful, and dance-like movements that resemble a slow-motion ballet. It generally takes about fifteen or twenty minutes to complete, depending on whether the long or short form is performed. Like the breathing exercises described in Chapter 8, T'ai Chi works by establishing and deepening our sense of contact with the physical, mental, and spiritual aspects of our being, and bringing these into harmony. Thus, T'ai Chi deserves careful attention by all persons who seek to enhance their sense of self-worth.

Many current books describe how to practice T'ai Chi. Generally, these contain photographs and/or diagrams that illustrate its many dance-like poses and a verbal description of the body movements involved. However, words and pictures cannot really capture the essence of T'ai Chi. Its practice consists not so much in individual positions as in the integration of these positions into a single, smoothly flowing motion—and the corresponding experience of our life energy through the physical motions. To learn T'ai Chi, we need a reliable teacher who can teach us either individually or in a group. Thus, rather than writing about how to perform the exercise, I am interested here in discussing the art's unique flavor and the ways it can enhance our physical, mental, and spiritual functioning, and thus exert a potent influence in strengthening our self-worth.

On one level, T'ai Chi is clearly a physical exercise, and on that level, it is a marvelous means of body discipline. It does not help us develop bigger muscles, but rather works toward softening and releasing muscular tension. T'ai Chi can also help us develop a fine-tuned awareness of our body and teach us grace, an elegant sense of balance, better posture, and a sense of pleasure and confidence in our physical being.

The introduction to the book *Embrace Tiger, Return to Mountain*, by T'ai Chi master Al Huang, contains this description of T'ai Chi's benefits:

> Tai ji is a subtle and powerful awareness discipline, a tool to become more in touch with yourself. It is a way of allowing yourself to function naturally and smoothly, uncluttered with expectations, shoulds, hopes, fears, and other fantasies that interfere with our natural flow. Unlike so many paths to awareness, tai ji is beautiful to experience as you do it, and also beautiful to watch from the outside. [Tai ji teaches that] if I am balanced *now*, then I can move in any direction I wish with no danger of falling. My contact with you is solid and real, coming to you from the root of my living. (pp. 7-8)

Later in the book, Al Huang writes of T'ai Chi:

> Insecurity and uncertainty are everywhere. If you don't let them become part of your flow, you will always be resisting and fighting. If the ground here suddenly shakes and trembles, can you *give* with it and still maintain your center? The joy in surfing and skiing and so many other sports is being able to do this. If you stiffen up and fight the wave, then you will never learn; you have to give in to the waves in order to ride them. If you can become fluid and open even when you are standing still, then this fluidness and openness

> [enables] you to respond to changes. You will be able to play with the changes and enjoy them. (p. 178)

## BUILDING SELF-WORTH THROUGH MARTIAL ARTS

During the past few years, I have utilized martial arts as a powerful adjunct to my therapeutic work. For example, Michael, twenty-six, initially complained to me that he had never succeeded at anything. He recognized that he thwarted his own efforts at success and that his daily moods alternated between being depressed and being "spaced out." Michael felt that he just could never "get it together" when it came to relating to others. He had been in psychotherapy previously for several years without benefiting much from the experience.

The treatment program that I set up for Michael was multifaceted, including both psychotherapy and the regular practice of T'ai Chi. It was not until he began practicing T'ai Chi that Michael became enthusiastic about his future. For the first time as an adult, he began to believe that he could succeed in life. He remarked about his daily T'ai Chi regimen, "Whenever I start 'spacing out' anymore, I make myself to into a T'ai Chi consciousness. It brings me right back to other people. I have never experienced anything so powerful. I tune in to 'me,' I become 'me' and not just a creature that reacts to its environment. I feel as though I get in touch with my true essence."

The overall gains that regular practice of T'ai Chi can bring to our body and mind are so well recognized that many hospitals and convalescent centers in China and Russia teach these methods to patients as a way to accelerate the healing process. In these countries, too, articles frequently appear in medical journals describing the healing benefits of T'ai Chi. I have likewise found in my medical practice that using T'ai Chi as a therapeutic aid for people with physical or emotional problems is a worthwhile aspect of patient care.

For example, Robin, thirty-two, came to me with several medical complaints, including an irregular heartbeat. Although her other ailments disappeared with the treatment I recommended, her heart irregularity continued and did not respond to conventional treatment. However, when Robin began practicing T'ai Chi for reasons unrelated to her medical condition, her irregular heartbeat was completely cured.

Certainly, isolated cases such as Michael's or Robin's can be explained away as coincidence. But I have witnessed many such cases and thousands of others have been reported by therapists and physicians around the globe. Although I was initially surprised when I learned of such instances, these clinical histories would come as no shock to health practitioners trained in the concepts of life energy and its significant connection to our well-being.

The relationship of T'ai Chi to our health has several additional aspects. Earlier in this chapter, I suggested an analogy between the circulation of blood in our arteries and veins and the circulation of chi in meridians throughout our body. Just as the blood circulation system has a center called the heart, so too the chi circulation system has a center called the *Tan T'ien* (pronounced "Dan Tien"), which means "field of energy." Located in the center of our body, approximately one to two inches below the naval, the Tan T'ien has also commonly been called the "one point," "hara," "kath," or simply the "center." This vital point is a reservoir of chi and serves, as does the heart, to facilitate the distribution of chi around the body.

The movements of the T'ai Chi exercise are a way to choreograph the flow of life energy along the pathways of the body, as well as a means of stimulating the circulation of chi along these pathways and between our body and our environment. Thus, T'ai Chi can do for our chi system what jogging can do for our cardiovascular system. Just as jogging can enhance and maintain the strength of our heart and circulatory system, so too can T'ai Chi increase the integrity of the life energy system. Since the chi system is believed to hold the key to health and illness, it seems reasonable that T'ai Chi can be effectively recommended for ailing individuals and all those wishing to better their health and vitality.

Throughout the ages, stories have been told of healers who have possessed remarkable power over illness. According to the tenets of T'ai Chi, every human being is capable of storing, concentrating, and directing chi. This highly focused chi is a tremendous healing force; great healers can channel this universal energy into others.

T'ai Chi has been extolled for more than its physical benefits. It has also long been venerated for its spiritual power. How can this be? Simply put, T'ai Chi is, in effect, a potent form of daily meditation as well as a concrete means of heightening our awareness of our spiritual center and spiritual energy.

Da Liu was a Tai Chi master who taught in New York for many years. Credited with helping to introduce T'ai Chi to Americans, he wrote evocatively in *T'ai Chi Ch'uan and I Ching, A Choreography of Body and Mind:*

> [T'ai Chi] disciplines the body, teaches relaxation and clear-headedness, accustoms the student to regulated breathing, and demonstrates the circulation of *chi* by a

> method far more close to the real event of meditation than looking at diagrams or hearing oral descriptions. More than that, T'ai Chi Ch'uan gives something of the spirit of meditation: a spirit which, in our own overactive, anxiety-ridden lives, we seldom taste in day-to-day living—a spirit which promises a glimpse of peace beyond the scope of our present imagination or our ordinary understanding of the world. (p. 84)

Finally, and I believe of least importance, T'ai Chi is also a martial art. Nonetheless, its combative power is by no means negligible. Indeed, T'ai Chi is recognized throughout the Orient as among the highest—if not the highest—form of martial art. Generally, though, T'ai Chi masters do not emphasize the fighting aspects of their skills. Although the combative elements are deemphasized, they are integral to the T'ai Chi exercise, for each movement can be applied effectively in fighting.

In keeping with the Taoist philosophy of *yin* and *yang*—the polarity between opposites in the universe—the same chi which people can use for healing becomes a deadly energy when directed against an enemy in combat. In battle, a T'ai Chi practitioner does not use physical strength but rather relies solely on chi. It is precisely this factor that makes T'ai Chi a most effective martial art, and yet it is the least sought after form of martial art, probably because it does not provide a quick means of self-defense in a street fight. There are many other martial arts in which we can learn punches, kicks, and other aggressive techniques in considerably less time and with less dedication than it takes to learn the effective control and use of chi.

Nor is T'ai Chi the martial art of choice if we are interested in athletic physical contact or in attaining the recognition of earning a brown belt or black belt. T'ai Chi offers no "belts" or degrees. It is typically practiced alone and in slow motion. Even when practiced with another person, it is performed very slowly without throws or other maneuvers typically associated with martial arts. Since chi can be channeled, fast maneuvers are unnecessary. Moreover, it is central to T'ai Chi philosophy that we do not have the right to channel chi in a combative way until we have first learned to channel it for healing purposes.

The essence of T'ai Chi is to put us in touch with our creative process. When its practice captures this essence, we make meaningful contact with our sense of self-worth. If T'ai Chi is performed in a stiff, mechanical, or overly solemn manner, that essence is lost. For this reason, I stress again that it is vital to find reliable teachers, who can instruct as much by the way they live as by the way they teach. Practicing the exercise form is but one way of expressing the essence of T'ai Chi. To limit T'ai Chi to the practice of its movements is only to dilute its essence. To maintain its effectiveness for enhancing our self-worth, we must make it integral to our total lifestyle.

## AIKIDO: SWIFT COUSIN TO T'AI CHI

Just as there are many forms of meditation that lead to the same sense of harmony, so too many forms of martial arts can enhance our sense of self-worth. Among these is Aikido (pronounced "I-Key-Doe"), which means "the way to union with Ki." Ki is the Japanese equivalent term for chi. Based on sophisticated knowledge that was centuries old, the discipline of Aikido was developed during the early 1900s by Morihei Ueshiba. Although it follows a somewhat different path from T'ai Chi, its basic spirit is quite similar. Koichi Tohei, its foremost proponent and master teacher, writes in his book *Aikido in Daily Life:*

> Aikido is the spirit of love and protection for all things. (p. 107)
>
> It is discipline in learning the laws of the universal, training so as to match each raising of the hand, each outstretching of the foot to those laws, unifying body and spirit and constantly refining oneself as part of the universal. (p. 16)

As is true for the practice of T'ai Chi, our progress in Aikido is based on a combination of both our own commitment and our teacher's ability. Basic Aikido training focuses on increasing our ability to contact, increase, and direct our ki, and heightening our awareness of our center—the Tan T'ien or "one point," as it is termed in Aikido. Such training, known as ki development, requires a unification of body, mind, and spirit.

Aikido does not utilize a unified exercise form as does T'ai Chi. Rather, during each class, participants practice a series of isolated exercises one at a time, each aimed at aiding in the development of ki. Nor are Aikido movements performed in slow motion. Indeed, as their skill develops, practitioners are required to execute many movements at high speed. No attacking methods are taught in Aikido. Its martial teachings are wholly defensive and are ultimately a powerful means of applying or channeling ki. Unlike T'ai Chi, Aikido does have a grade or belt ranking system and emphasizes developing prowess in physical combat. However, there are no competitions or matches in Aikido. Competitive matches imply that someone wins and someone else loses, and this concept is foreign to the very basis of Aikido. To paraphrase Aikido master Tohei, opponents do not fight in Aikido. They work together in a spirit of mutual respect and love to correct each others' weak points and to help each other train their bodies, minds, and spirits towards a state of purity and love.

Aikido's fighting maneuvers involve keeping centered in our "one point" and directing ki rather than using brute strength. Therefore, the smoothness and apparent effortlessness with which Aikido is performed gives practitioners immediate feedback about their level of ki development. Such rapid feedback is extremely helpful as a teaching strategy. Aside from its self-defense applications, Aikido is also highly useful as a means of training people to focus their awareness on their centers and to project ki at all times and under any circumstances. A major aim of Aikido training is to bring people closer to using ki properly in all aspects of day-to-day life, including eating, walking, speaking, waking up, or even sleeping. Becoming centered in this manner leads to a strong sense of self-worth.

For those who choose the martial arts as a method to enhance self-worth, many will be attracted to the action and immediate feedback offered by Aikido. For some, the meditative effortlessness and graceful, flowing motions of T'ai Chi will be appealing. For others, a different form of the soft martial arts may be especially appropriate. People who practice any of these disciplines will find them a time-honored and trustworthy path toward enhancing self-worth.

## EXERCISES

The exercises described on the following pages have a powerful, often dramatic effect. I have demonstrated them many times. To place them in proper perspective, let us consider the effect of electricity, certainly a familiar form of energy, on a person who has never heard or seen such wizardry. No doubt, witnessing the effects of this power would be initially mind-boggling. Yet, most of us now take electricity for granted. It is obviously a question of what our particular culture highlights as important. For many peoples of the world, chi and its effects are as unquestionable as electricity is to us.

Like the reality of microbes before the advent of the microscope in the seventeenth century, subtle life energy is not yet an accepted part of Western culture. However, the concept of chi offers us an exciting new way of expanding our view of ourselves and our universe, and it connects directly to the development of our sense of self-worth. The more time and attention you give these exercises, the greater the rewards.

Although T'ai Chi and Aikido movements can be recorded on paper, written instructions—which tell you where to place your feet or how to hold your hands —can describe only the surface level of the exercise. At best, they can be useful reminders to those who wish to review what they have learned from their teachers. Moreover, written instructions alone cannot give the uninitiated an adequate sense of what these formidable disciplines are about.

Other exercises, however, that are relatively easy to perform, can give us an inkling of the life energy system within us. Chi cannot be seen any more than electricity can. But just as the effects of electricity can be observed, so too the effects of chi can be monitored.

The six exercises that follow can help to demonstrate this reality. The first two are procedures used as tests in ki development training, and the last four derive from the field of applied kinesiology. You will need a partner, preferably one whose strength is about equal to yours, to assist you in each of these exercises. Your partner's role is not as an opponent seeking to overpower or defeat you, but rather as a helper working with you for mutual benefit.

## *Exercise #1.*
## Becoming Aware of Your Center

STEP 1. Stand naturally with your feet apart about the width of your shoulders and parallel to each other. Your partner, using the fingertips, pushes against the mid-upper portion of your chest to determine how much force is needed to push you over. Your partner's task is neither to hurt you nor to employ excessive force, but rather to gauge the least amount of pressure necessary to push you off balance.

STEP 2. After your partner has determined this amount during several tries, resume your initial stance. But now, as best as you can, focus all your attention on your "one point," located about two inches below your naval. It may help your concentration to hold one of your fingertips on this spot. When you are focused, have your partner try to push you over once again (as in Step 1). Make no conscious attempt to resist the push. Indeed, try not to think about it, as you focus only on your one point.

COMMENTS Teaching students to focus consciously on their one point is a method used in Aikido training to help beginners develop an awareness of their center. The more you are able to focus and sustain your attention on your one point, the more stable you become. The force your partner needed previously to move you will not budge you while you are centered. The object of this introductory exercise is not to transform you into an immovable object, but rather to demonstrate that you become significantly more stable and able to withstand significantly more force when you are in touch with your center.

Your increased stability in Step 2 is not merely a function of the fact that you are mobilizing your attention. To prove this, repeat Step 2 but instead of focusing on your one point, concentrate instead on a spot in the middle of your forehead or any other body region. You will likely discover that you gain the maximum amount of stability when you focus on your one point.

## *Exercise #2.* Aikido Unbending Arm

STEP 1. Extend your arm in front of you with your thumb facing up and your elbow slightly bent. Keep your arm as strong as you can make it. Your partner then grasps the underside of your extended wrist with one hand, presses on your upper arm (over your bicep muscle) with the other hand, and attempts to bend your arm back toward your shoulder. Your partner should use strength, applying it with steadily increasing pressure rather than with a sudden jerk of force. Using your strength, try to keep your arm from being bent back. if the two of you are of equal strength, or if your partner is stronger, your partner will probably experience little difficulty in bending your arm. However, as in the first exercise, it is not your partner's role to overwhelm you but rather to determine the least amount of force necessary to bend your arm.

STEP 2. Extend your arm in front of you as before, but this time do not tense your muscles. Allow your arm to stay relaxed (which is not the same as being collapsed), focus your attention on your one point, and imagine that at this spot inside your body is an energy generator more powerful than a nuclear reactor. Also

imagine that you can direct this energy at will and send it up through your belly and chest to the shoulder of your outstretched arm, and then right through your arm and out the fingertips.

It may be helpful to think of a fire hose. When not in use, a fire hose is soft and pliable, but when water flows through it under pressure, the hose becomes hard and strong. The hose does not gain its strength by tightening up, but becomes strong by allowing the water to flow uninhibitedly.

Now, imagine that your arm is hollow like a fire hose and let the powerful energy from your center flow through your arm and shoot out of your hand with such force that it could travel for thousands of miles. Your fingers are like the nozzle and they direct the energy. Point them straight ahead.

Once again, your partner tries to bend your arm back using strength. It is important that you keep your arm relaxed and maintain the fire hose image in your mind. Avoid flexing your muscles against your partner's physical pressure. The more you can do this, the more unbending your arm becomes. The same amount of force that your partner used previously to bend your arm will no longer be enough to bend it.

By keeping one hand on your bicep, your partner will be able to tell whether you are tensing your muscles. Consequently, your partner can help you by telling you when your muscles begin to tighten. This can help both of you to understand that there is a force within you that is neither dependent on nor limited to your muscular structure for its power.

COMMENTS In Aikido training, practicing this exercise is a way of helping students to develop awareness of the presence and potency of the life energy that flows in their bodies. It is also a striking demonstration that by staying relaxed and utilizing their ki, they have far greater strength than they could possibly muster by using merely muscular power. Indeed, the more they tense their muscles, the less strength they possess.

This exercise can be confused with the unbendable arm demonstration commonly employed by stage hypnotists. In actuality, there are two very different processes at work. Using hypnosis, it is certainly possible to suggest successfully to a "good" subject that his or her arm is as strong as a lead pipe which cannot be bent. In my opinion, hypnosis can be a very effective therapeutic tool. It can indeed make an individual's arm strong. However, Aikido does not use trance-like states; nor does it encourage students to make their bodies rigid and tense. No trance state is necessary in ki training; the key image is one of relaxation. The arm remains slightly bent and the muscles stay soft and unflexed.

The next exercises derive from a field of study known as Applied Kinesiology, developed by Dr. George Goodheart. It is used primarily as a method of diagnosing and treating illness. However, since this field of medicine is based partly on the concept of a life energy system, some of its discoveries are relevant to this chapter. I have abstracted four of these discoveries, somewhat out of their original context, and I present them as exercises that demonstrate other effects of the life energy system.

## *Exercise #3.* Chi Arm Strength

STEP 1. Have your partner extend one arm straight out with the palm down in front of the body. Stand facing your partner's outstretched arm (on the thumb side) and place your hand on the wrist. Tell your partner to keep the arm up despite the fact that you are about to try forcing it down by pressing on the wrist. Your partner's task is to try to resist your downward force; your task is to continue to slowly increase that force to gauge how much pressure you need to push the arm down.

This is not an arm wrestling contest, and you are not competing with one another. Rather, you are working together to determine the amount of strength or resistance in your partner's arm. To accomplish this, use the least amount of force necessary to push your partner's arm down. You might use just one finger if you are doing this exercise with a child or both hands if you are working with someone considerably stronger than yourself.

STEP 2. Having made the determination described in Step 1, carry out the following maneuver, and then retest your partner's arm to see if there is a change in his or her ability to resist a similar amount of force. Place your hand over your partner's thumbnail, and slide your hand up your partner's arm, proceeding in a straight line from the thumb to the shoulder. Then from the shoulder, slide your hand down onto his or her chest some two or three inches. Repeat this maneuver two or three times, and then retest your partner's arm (as in Step 1).

STEP 3. Reverse the line traced by your hand. Start at the chest and end at the thumb. Repeat this motion two or three times, and then retest your partner's arm (as in Step 1). In most cases, you will notice a significant decrease in your partner's strength when you follow the procedure in Step 2, and a return to the original strength, or even a greater strength in Step 3. For some people, this result is reversed; they become stronger with Step 2 and weaker with Step 3.

COMMENTS Although these results may seem like magic, there is no trick involved. Earlier in this chapter, we discussed the ancient Eastern idea that chi flows through the body in channels called meridians. In this exercise, you are using your hand to trace one of the meridians, specifically, the lung meridian. The energy flows through each meridian in only one direction; in the case of the lung meridian, chi flows from the upper chest to the end of the thumb. From there it moves to another meridian and continues its journey through the body.

It is possible to use your own energy field to influence another person's field. Thus, by placing and moving your hand over your partner's meridian, you will temporarily influence the flow of energy along that meridian. When you move your hand *against* the flow (from thumb to chest), you temporarily impede it. The degree of impedance depends on the force of your energy and your partner's energy, and is unrelated to the muscular strength of either partner. When the flow of chi decreases, strength correspondingly diminishes, though no change is noticeable in the muscles.

When you move your hand *with* the flow of energy (chest to thumb), you temporarily enhance the chi flow, and with it strength returns to the arm. In some cases where an impedance to chi exists already, your motion may temporarily help overcome it. In this instance, your partner's arm may become significantly stronger than it was in Step 1.

In some people, a condition known as "switching" exists, which causes the chi to flow in a reverse pattern. This condition can produce a variety of symptoms, such as difficulty in left/right discrimination. When an individual is switched, he or she will exhibit increased strength during Step 2 and diminished strength during Step 3. By stimulating other meridian pathways, it is possible to similarly strengthen other parts of a person's body.

The next two exercises are among many that help demonstrate the effects of environmental materials on the flow of chi in our body and the amount of life energy available to us.

## *Exercise #4.* Lead and Chi Arm Strength

STEP 1. Follow the same procedure as in Step 1 of Exercise #3.

STEP 2. Get a square piece of lead about one and one-half to two inches on each side. These are generally available from plumbing supply stores. Have your partner hold this square against his or her lips for a few seconds. The mouth should be closed. While your partner is doing this, retest the strength of his or her arm.

STEP 3. Remove the lead. Wait a few seconds, then retest.

COMMENTS Many people experience a marked decrease in personal strength when their lips are covered with a lead square. This is because lead and other materials interfere somewhat with the flow of chi. When the lead is pressed against the lips, the flow of chi in two meridians is hindered.

This hindrance decreases the overall chi available to the body and results in diminished strength. When a person is highly charged with chi, the decrease caused by the lead will not be significant enough to affect strength. However, when a person's chi is weaker, lead can cause a marked decrease of strength.

## *Exercise #5.* Jewelry and Chi Arm Strength

STEP 1. Have your partner extend his or her left arm straight in front. Test your partner's strength as in Step 2 of Exercise #3.

STEP 2. Have your partner hold an open safety pin between two fingers of the extended left hand. Then retest your partner's strength.

STEP 3. Follow the same procedure as in Step 2, except keep the safety pin closed.

STEP 4. Repeat Steps 1, 2 and 3, using your partner's right arm.

COMMENTS In most instances, you will find that when your partner holds the safety pin in the left hand, there is a noticeable decrease in strength when the pin is open, and no decrease in strength when the pin is closed. However, when the pin is held in the right hand, there will generally be no effect on your partner's level of strength, regardless of whether the pin is open or closed.

The explanation for the different results on the left and right sides of the body lies in the intricate pathways for chi flow. Metal and other substances that make a complete ring will usually not adversely effect chi flow. However, a broken ring of metal can interfere with the flow of energy if it is placed at specific points.

It is likewise possible for a wide variety of objects with which we have prolonged contact, such as jewelry and particularly wristwatches (because of their moving parts or chemical batteries) to hinder chi flow. Testing our strength in the manner described above while wearing jewelry or a wristwatch and while the jewelry or wristwatch is removed can be a valuable way of determining what, if any, effect such objects have on the vitality of our life energy.

## *Exercise #6.*
## Marching and Chi Arm Strength

STEP 1. Follow the same procedure as in Step 1 of Exercise #4.

STEP 2. Have your partner march in place in such a manner that each time the right leg lifts the right arm lifts as well. The same should be true of the left arm and leg. After your partner marches in this manner for thirty to sixty seconds, retest the arm muscles.

STEP 3. Have your partner march in place once more, but this time the right arm lifts each time the left leg is lifted. Likewise, the left arm lifts each time the right leg is lifted. After thirty to sixty seconds of marching, retest the muscle.

COMMENTS You will typically discover that your partner is weaker when he or she follows Step 2 and stronger when following Step 3. For most people, the cross-crawl pattern (Step 3-type marching or walking) correlates with the normal flow of chi, while the non-crossed pattern (as in Step 2) interferes with the chi flow. In this regard, T'ai Chi can be seen as a most sophisticated method of enhancing the flow of our own chi.

# 8

# The Breath of Life

*And the lord God formed the man of dust from the ground and breathed into his nostrils the breath of life; and the man became a living being.*

Genesis II:7

The very ordinariness of breathing makes us likely to ignore this vital function. To breathe freely again after an illness that has restricted our breathing, even a mere head cold, often feels positively exhilarating. Soon, however, we lose this wonderful awareness. As we resume our normal routine, the inherent, sensual pleasure and beauty of each breath fades from our consciousness. This reaction is hardly surprising in our technological society; free from immediate pain or discomfort, we invariably dissociate ourselves from body awareness. In our frantic pursuit of external goals, we seldom think of our physical functioning at all.

We must be reminded that the specific quality of our breathing affects strongly how alive we feel. I believe that this principle applies not only to our physical nature, but to our emotional and spiritual energies as well. Thus proper breathing is essential to fostering and maintaining a strong sense of self-worth.

On philosophical grounds as well, breathing warrants significant attention. Historically, the world's great spiritual traditions have always recognized the central importance of breathing. In his book *Creative Meditation and Multi-Dimensional Consciousness*, the modern Tibetan monk Lama Anagarika Govinda aptly observed: "The process of breathing if fully understood and experienced in its profound significance, could teach us more than all the philosophies of the world." (p. 120)

This bold statement can be supported by the universal lessons we can learn from breathing. First, breathing is a vivid example of our interdependence with the environment. Human beings need the oxygen that plants produce, and we in turn provide plants with life-sustaining carbon dioxide. Moreover, the act of breathing is a common denominator we share with all life forms; the breathing motion of expansion and contraction is basic to even single-celled organisms. Breathing can also teach us the symbolic importance of letting go; for no matter how essential air is to our survival, holding onto the air we inhale swiftly leads to death. Thus, breathing demonstrates that releasing is as crucial to life as taking in.

From a strictly biologic viewpoint, the process of respiration is the most important of all body functions. We can survive for only a few minutes without inhaling oxygen and exhaling carbon dioxide. Moreover, this vital exchange of gases is only one of many physical functions which depend on breathing. That is, the *quality* of our breathing greatly affects the efficient operation of other body systems which depend on oxygen, and correspondingly, affects the nature of our day-to-day life.

Proper digestion, for example, is influenced by the quality of our breathing. In order to benefit nutritionally from foods and beverages we consume, our food must first be mixed with oxygen. Our digestive organs themselves also require oxygen in order to function. When we breathe improperly, we provide insufficient oxygen, resulting in poor digestion, no matter what we eat. I have seen patients who, despite good diets and appropriate vitamin and mineral supplements, continue to suffer from nutritional deficiencies because of their chronically poor breathing habits. When such individuals are taught to breathe properly, their health problems promptly disappear.

Our physical energy also depends on the burning or oxygenation of food. If we lack sufficient oxygen, we are likely to suffer from chronic fatigue and exhaustion. If this sounds familiar, you should assess your breathing: Is your respiratory system working at less than optimum efficiency? A helpful way to perform this evaluation is described in Exercise #1 in this chapter.

Body heat is similarly determined by proper oxygenation. Insufficient oxygen can make us feel cold and consequently intolerant of cold weather. To make this idea clear, think of a blacksmith who wants to make his fire hotter. He does not add coal or wood to the fire. Instead, he uses his bellows to add air. In my clinical experience, I have found that people who suffer habitually from low energy caused by poor oxygenation benefit tremendously by learning how to breathe more effectively.

Our breathing also serves to exercise major internal organs. That is, the mechanical action of the diaphragm moving down and up gently massages our liver, stomach, spleen, intestines, and other organs. All organs need exercise in order to function optimally, and proper breathing plays a vital role in this natural function. An organ that is not regularly exercised is less efficient and more susceptible to illness. Eventually, poor breathing can lead to many chronic diseases, not ordinarily associated with respiration. Likewise, improper breathing can make us vulnerable to a variety of respiratory ailments.

In short, breathing is vital for the maintenance of our well-being and vitality.

## MIND AND BODY

Just as correct breathing is necessary for our physical health, so too our emotional well-being is linked to the way we breathe. In recent years, psychotherapeutic treatment methods have begun to address the connections between human personality and body-energy processes including breathing. These approaches emphasize the importance of locating and experiencing hidden emotional conflicts *within the body*, instead of simply discussing or analyzing them. They also incorporate insights about body language as a key to our emotional makeup, and, to varying degrees, they utilize massage and movement techniques to release the feelings which lie hidden in our musculature. Among the most cohesive of these systems is Bioenergetic Analysis, developed by Dr. Alexander Lowen and Dr. John Pierrakos. Historically, most studies of human personality in mainstream psychology have focused on the importance of the mind, and ignored the body. A fundamental tenet of Bioenergetic Analysis, however, is that we cannot truly separate mind and body. Dr. Lowen has cogently observed:

> [Our body] has a motility independent of ego control which is manifested by the spontaneity of its gestures

> and the vivacity of its expression. It hums, it vibrates, it glows. It is charged with feeling. The first difficulty that one encounters with patients in search of identity is that they are not aware of the lack of aliveness in their bodies.

In practical terms, this principle means that our personality is expressed as much through our body as through our mind. Sigmund Freud was well aware of this connection, as evidenced by his classic observation that ego is first and foremost body ego. But Freud never carried this insight to the logical conclusion of working with the body to influence the ego. As a result, many psychotherapists deal with body sensations and feelings only superficially. This tendency stems from conceptualizing the body and mind as two wholly separate entities.

Yet, a moment's reflection will reveal that expressing feelings or thoughts always requires body movement. Intense emotions such as anger and love are expressed through voice, facial expression, gestures, and actions. Similarly, the act of *holding back* a feeling or thought—for instance, not saying "I am angry" or "I love you"—necessitates tightening or contracting part of our body in some way. In exactly the same manner, expressing an emotional conflict or any character trait requires that we use our body.

We are all aware that the human body "speaks" a language, and to varying degrees, we all know how to read that language. Cross-cultural expressions such as eye contact, tone of voice, gait, stance, style of handshake, position of jaw or shoulders, and spontaneity and ease of movement all give us clues about what another person is experiencing. Thus, we are usually aware when a friend is angry simply by the way she is sitting. Or, by the way an acquaintance steps into a room, we can often tell that he is elated about something.

Poets, novelists, and artists have always called our attention to such details. Acting teachers rely on such insights to train aspiring thespians. A common teaching method is to ask a student to express a variety of emotions or nuances by saying a simple phrase, such as "It's raining." Just as actors can convey passion, boredom, or even utter despair by the way they say such a phrase, each of us expresses emotional states without thinking by our tones, inflections, and body movements. Practitioners like Dr. Lowen and his colleagues have made the language of the body a legitimate field of psychological inquiry and therapy.

The body speaks a language in every pose and every gesture. It does so in obvious ways that most of us easily recognize, as well as in subtle ways that most of us miss—unless we devote time to studying the intricacies of this nonverbal language. Each person expresses himself or herself as a unity. It is not our mind that becomes angry, nor our body that strikes. Rather, it is always one's complete bodymind that expresses itself. As a general rule, *one cannot affect the mind without affecting the body, nor can one affect the body without affecting the mind.*

## BREATHING: GATEWAY TO SENSUAL PLEASURE

In a similar way, our capacity for pleasure and our ability to resist depression and anxiety depend on how we are in the world physically and emotionally, the degree of aliveness in our bodies and minds. When we take both our bodies and our feelings into consideration, we are more likely to be able to make lasting changes in our life. In this regard, Dr. Lowen observes in his book *Pleasure:*

> The two functions that are most important . . . are *breathing* and *movement*. Both of these functions are disturbed in every person who has an emotional conflict by chronic muscular tensions that are the physical counterpart of psychological conflicts. Through these muscular tensions conflicts become structured in the body. (pp. 36–7)

My experience with patients seeking psychiatric help corroborates Dr. Lowen's view. I have found that working with my patients' breathing and movement in conjunction with their mental states is a more effective therapeutic approach than working only with what they say about themselves.

What we feel and how much we feel are determined largely by the quality of our breathing. Strong emotions stimulate us to breathe deeply. The reverse is also true: breathing deeply enables us to experience strong emotions.

Holding our breath is an effective way to stop a feeling from revealing itself. We generally hold our breath unconsciously, though at times we may be aware of doing it. During childhood, when we were told not to scream, we tightened our throats. We learned to restrain angry impulses by tightening our chests and holding our shoulders back. To suppress tears of sadness or hurt, we likewise learned to swallow hard and hold our breath.

Each of these body movements hinders respiration. The more fearful we are of feelings, such as anger, sadness, or even fear itself, the more we restrain our breathing. This restraint limits our capacity to experience a full range of human emotions deeply.

Many people hold their breath at least momentarily when they experience any kind of stress. They do so out of habit, though ironically the effect of their action is to increase their stress. By contrast, taking a deep breath at a moment of stress reduces tension. If you pay attention to this aspect of your behavior, you may be surprised to discover how many times each day you suddenly hold your breath. Each time you hold your breath during a stressful episode, you increase your degree of physical and emotional tension.

However, you can always change if you become more self-aware. When you find that you are holding your breath, you will probably notice that you have also tightened part of your body as well. During such moments, practice releasing the tightness and breathing deeply. In this way, you can diminish some of the stress you have inadvertently created in yourself.

Breathing improperly can also exacerbate a variety of emotional symptoms including restlessness, irritability, poor concentration, depression, anxiety, and tension. Similarly, sexual dissatisfaction can be related to, and aggravated by, poor breathing habits, particularly holding the breath just before or at the moment of climax.

Of course, at times we may curtail our breathing because we have an underlying fear of sexual feeling, just as we hold our breath when we experience any strong feeling that we want to repress. This tendency necessitates a cautionary word. As I mentioned earlier, stimulating and deepening our breathing may cause us to experience powerful and intense emotions. Consequently, any feelings that we have long suppressed may suddenly erupt when we deliberately stimulate our breathing.

I have often witnessed this dramatic phenomenon, which can include sudden outbursts of crying or laughing, or intense feelings of anger or jealousy. At times, these powerful eruptions flow from the release of memories of specific occasions when we felt embarrassment, humiliation, fear, or pain. In other instances, no particular images or mental associations surface in the individual's mind. Because such an eruption may arise during directed breathing, I always alert my patients. Generally, the sudden release of suppressed emotions is best done in a place where the person feels safe and in the presence of someone trustworthy and knowledgeable about such reactions. Even when a suitable therapist is available, I do not typically recommend deep breathing as a technique for those who already have difficulty restraining their emotions. This is because such persons need to gain other strengths first, such as the ability to moderate their emotional reactions.

## BREATHING: THE SPIRITUAL CONNECTION

As discussed in Chapter 7, spiritual adepts around the world have taught for centuries that a special kind of energy (yet undiscovered by modern physics) is present in all things. This energy is most concentrated in living beings. Different cultures have given different names to it, including chi, ki, prana, and ruach, but the overall description remains essentially the same, no matter what name it is given.

This force is a universal energy, and all other forms of energy are derivations or manifestations of it. For our purposes, we can simply describe this force as "life energy." The ancient traditions teach that we absorb a certain amount of life energy with each breath, and that with conscious breathing, we can increase the amount of life energy we absorb. This energy can be stored within the body. Just as oxygen is vital to the functioning of our physical body, this energy is essential to the healthy functioning of our spiritual body. For example, Hindu sages have taught that the life energy, which they call prana, is found in its freest state in air, and that we absorb it into our bodies more easily from air than from any other source.

In recent years, scientists have tried to prove that air is indeed filled, or charged, with some previously unknown form of energy. Among these was psychiatrist Wilhelm Reich, who conducted research in this field. At the time of his death in 1957, Reich felt that he had discovered proof of a life force that he termed "orgone" energy. Reich has loyal adherents to this day, but his orgone studies are still outside the bounds of conventional science. More recently, a number of similar claims have been made by Soviet scientists, who call their discovery "bioplasma." However, details of such work remain obscure, and to date, no chemical or physical evidence has been discovered to convince mainstream science.

In the absence of scientific proof, we are left with an ancient and enduring belief in both East and West that a universal, life-enhancing energy is in the air we breathe. Is this belief a universal truth which, like the reality of microbes, awaits the discovery of an instrument to validate it? Or were our ancestors embracing a myth? Although I may have no convincing proof, I choose to accept the notion of life energy. For me, it is a useful concept that helps explain many things.

If we choose to believe, or are at least receptive to this intriguing notion, we have even more reason to develop proper breathing habits. Even without the idea of life energy, it seems apparent that proper breathing is crucial to our overall well-being. The more alive we feel, the better our health; the more in touch we are with our being, the greater will be our resulting self-worth.

## RESTORING HEALTHY BREATHING

When we first come into this world, we need no instruction on how to breathe. Physically healthy infants breathe properly and do so spontaneously. Generally, they continue to do so unless something interferes with this natural process. It hardly seems coincidental that once children begin internalizing a host of "shoulds" and "should nots," they characteristically shift towards restricted breathing. This is particularly true when the rules children internalize involve a denial or suppression of normal emotions. To this day, most of us can probably recall being admonished, "You shouldn't cry." or "Big girls don't feel this way." or "You should be happy. Stop whining like that!" or "Don't be a crybaby!"

As children grow older, they begin to value self-control. In time, restricted breathing becomes a way of life. By the time we reach adulthood, most of us need specific guidance to learn to breathe properly. Indeed, some people even joke about not having enough time during the day to breathe.

In my work as a physician, I have observed that the two most prevalent breathing problems in our society are: 1) mouth breathing; and 2) incomplete breathing. Both of these problems are correctible, and the benefits of correcting them are worth the effort involved.

It is usually more healthful to inhale through our nose than our mouth. Our nasal passageways alter the air we breathe in two important ways: first, by serving as a filter to remove particles of dust, dirt, as well as germs and other impurities that might otherwise make their way into our lungs; and second, by warming the air and thereby preventing cold air from entering our lungs directly. Our lungs work less efficiently and can even be damaged when they are continually exposed to impurities and cold air. Such exposure occurs when we breathe in through our mouth, since the mouth neither filters nor warms the air as efficiently as the nose. Also, some physicians believe that chronic mouth breathing increases the likelihood of our developing respiratory diseases.

Some people who regularly breathe through their nose while awake nevertheless breathe through their mouth while asleep. They often awaken in the morning with a dry mouth or a parched throat. Mouth breathing can also often lead to congested nasal passages, because when nasal passageways are not used, they tend to clog up. Consequently, when a chronically stuffed nose forces us to breathe through our mouth, we may need professional help before we can reestablish normal nasal breathing.

The second common breathing problem is incomplete breathing. Unfortunately, this problem is currently so widespread that it has become the "normal" mode of respiration. Most people who breathe in this ineffective manner are not aware that it restricts them physically, nor that it hinders their sense of self-worth. Nor do they realize that alternatives to shallow breathing do exist.

Incomplete or restricted breathing occurs when we use the muscles of respiration that expand and contract our chest cavity partially rather than fully. Our breathing can similarly be limited when our respiratory muscles work against each other rather than as a team.

In the next section of this chapter, I present a variety of exercises designed to correct these two common difficulties. If you practice them regularly, you will discover how powerfully they enhance your emotional and physical vitality. Your sense of self-worth will substantially increase too, because simply *being* in the world—just breathing the air around you—becomes a pleasurable and satisfying experience.

## BREATHING EXERCISES

### *Preliminary Exercise:* Assessing Your Breathing

You can assess your own breathing pattern by following three steps.

STEP 1. Place your hands on your abdomen. Observe whether it moves as you breathe in and out. If it does move, note how much it moves and whether it moves in or out as you inhale and exhale.

The movement of the belly is related to the upward and downward movement of the diaphragm, the major muscle of breathing. By noting how much your belly moves, you can assess how well you are using your major muscle of respiration. If you detect little movement, you are barely using your diaphragm, and your breathing is incomplete. If your belly does move, check to see if its movement enhances or restricts your respiration.

When your belly moves out as you breathe in, and moves in as you breathe out, your breath is more complete. This is our "natural" way to breathe, the way we breathe at birth and during infancy, until social pressure forces us to inhibit our breathing. Ironically, for most people, natural breathing often feels abnormal at first.

If you find that your belly moves in the reverse manner—in, as you breathe in, and out, as you breathe out

—you are probably restricting your breathing. If your belly moves in when you inhale, your diaphragm is moving up into your chest cavity, compressing your lung space and forcing air out. Thus, you are working against yourself: one part of your breathing apparatus is sucking air in, while another part is simultaneously pushing air out. This inefficiency leads to incomplete breath.

STEP 2. Place your hands on your chest wall just below and slightly to the outside of your breasts. Observe whether your rib cage moves. If it does, observe the degree of its movement as you breathe in and out.

In addition to the diaphragm, intercostal muscles located between the ribs aid in respiration by expanding and contracting the rib cage. As the rib cage expands, the chest cavity increases, and air is sucked into the lungs. As the rib cage contracts, the chest cavity is compressed, and air is forced out of the lungs. If your rib cage hardly moves, you are probably breathing incorrectly.

STEP 3. Place your fingers under your collar bones and observe whether this part of your chest moves

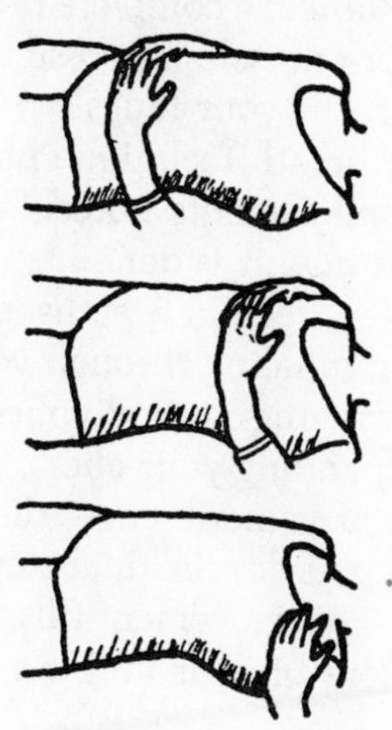

when you breathe. Observe the extent of its movement as you breathe in and out.

This step is actually an extension of Step 2. It assesses the function of the uppermost and smallest portion of your lungs. Minimal movement of this part of your chest is additional evidence of incomplete breathing. Conversely, breathing confined only to this area is the most inefficient type of breathing.

If any of the three steps above reveals your breathing to be restricted, you should practice developing a more complete breath unless you have a mechanical blockage. The exercises in this section are designed to accomplish this goal.

## *Exercise #1.* Yogic Complete Breath

Yogis have always stressed the importance of proper breathing and have developed many breathing exercises to achieve this end. The most basic one is known as the "complete breath." A complete breath is not measured by how fully you fill your lungs, as it is possible to take a complete breath while inhaling a small amount of air. Rather, a complete breath uses as many of your respiratory muscles as possible, and distributes the air to all parts of your lungs.

The complete breath technique blends in a flowing manner all the movements noted in the Preliminary Exercise. Here is how it is done:

STEP 1. Take a few related breaths, ending with a full exhalation. Then inhaling through your nose, fill your lungs by first bringing your diaphragm down (belly out), then by expanding your chest, and finally by expanding the top of your rib cage, the area under your collar bones. As you do this final step, your belly will move in a little. This movement fills the lower, middle and upper portions of your lungs in turn.

STEP 2. Hold your breath for a few seconds. Then begin your exhalation, breathing out slowly through your nose. First let your belly come in, forcing the air out of your lungs. Then, let your chest relax, starting with the portion under the collar bone and working down to the lower part of your chest and abdomen. Again, hold your breath for a few seconds.

Although I have by necessity described this exercise step-by-step, each inhalation and exhalation should have a unified, flowing, wavelike motion. However, it may take practice to achieve this coordination. I recommend that you practice this breathing exercise while in sitting, standing, and supine positions, so that you develop proficiency in each. Lying down, or supine, is usually the easiest.

It takes considerable practice to change your breathing patterns, but with gentle effort, you can reestablish the complete breath as your dominant mode. However, even before this occurs, you can benefit from a complete expansion of your lungs and respiratory muscles by doing a series of complete breaths a few times every day.

A yawn is nature's way of forcing us to take a complete breath when our breathing pattern has become especially poor and inefficient. By observing your belly and chest movements when you yawn, you will see how your body moves during a complete breath. A major difference between a yawn and a complete breath, however, is that during the yawn you breathe through your mouth. As we have noted, mouth breathing can occur spontaneously when your need for oxygen increases, as it does after strenuous exercise or, in the case of a yawn, when your breathing has not supplied enough oxygen. Thus, while a yawn can instruct you, it may also be a reminder that you have been breathing incorrectly.

I have observed two common difficulties when people try to perform this exercise. First, you may be unable to get your belly to move in proper rhythm with your breathing. To solve this problem try performing the exercise while lying on your back. This modification is frequently enough to get your breathing on the right track.

When this position does not solve the problem, forceably exhale all the air you can while pressing your fists into your abdomen. This action pushes the belly in on the exhalation. If you hold your breath in this position, the inhalation that follows will spontaneously push your belly out. It may take several tries before the proper movements of the diaphragm get started. (On rare occasions you may need someone else to provide the necessary abdominal pressure.)

The second difficulty is that you may be unable to get the upper portion of your rib cage (the part under the collar bone) to expand at the end of inhalation. You can generally obtain a sense of what this movement is like by holding your diaphragm and some of your ribs, and sniffing through your nose in short, strong bursts. By raising your shoulders slightly toward the end of inhalation, you can better expand your collar bone area.

## *Exercise #2.* Yogic Complete Breath While Walking

This is a variation of the previous exercise. It combines the principles of the complete breath with the activity of walking. It is important that you walk with your body straight but not rigid, and that your steps follow a set rhythm.

Adjust the rhythm of your steps so that your inhalation—a complete breath—requires a fixed number of steps to complete and your exhalation can be completed in the same number of steps. Choose an even number of breaths and steps, such as four, six, or eight.

Then, counting to yourself, inhale for the appropriate number of steps. Hold your breath for half that number of steps. Then exhale for the required number of steps. Finally, hold your breath for half that number of steps. Repeat this cycle for the duration of the exercise.

## *Exercise #3.* Yogic Cleansing Breath

Yogis use this exercise to tone up their respiratory system and recharge body energy. Start by taking in a complete breath. Hold it for a few seconds. Then, before exhaling, form your lips into a whistling position without puffing up your cheeks.

With your lips pursed, exhale the air in a series of short, strong bursts through the small opening between your lips until your exhalation is complete. Pause between each burst. You can perform this exercise for a single breath or for a series of breaths.

The next three exercises come from Bioenergetic Analysis and are often used as part of the psychotherapeutic techniques of Bioenergetics. However, they like other Bioenergetics exercises can be practiced outside of psychotherapy to help increase a person's sense of aliveness and capacity for pleasure. Each of these exercises should be performed for one to several minutes.

## *Exercise #4.* Bow or Arch

Stand with your feet apart about the width of your shoulders. Your toes should be pointed somewhat towards each other (a slight pigeon-toed position). Bend your knees as much as possible, without leaning forward or lifting your heels off the floor. Form your hands into fists, and place them in the small of your back. Pull your elbows toward each other. Then arch your back over your fists, keeping your neck in line with your spine and your feet flat on the floor. Your weight should be primarily on the balls of your feet. Do not allow your head to fall back. Nor should you push your buttocks all the way forward or pull them back all the way.

Maintaining this position, inhale deeply through your nose, letting your belly come out as fully as possible. Hold your breath for a moment; then exhale slowly through your open mouth. Make a continual sound as you breathe out, such as "ahh," and continue the sound and exhalation for as long as you can.

Making sounds is directly related to breathing. The inhibition of sounds, particularly when such inhibitions become ingrained, restricts our respiration. For example, many people in our society find it difficult to cry, scream, shout, or laugh easily. Freeing our voice is an integral part of restoring complete breathing.

It is common when performing this exercise, or other bioenergetic exercises, to experience vibration in your legs or other parts of your body. These vibrations are generally not a reason to stop the exercise. Indeed, they can be quite invigorating. Tingling sensations in your body typically indicate that you are unaccustomed to breathing deeply. As you get used to deep breathing, the tingling tends to disappear.

However, if the tingling bothers you, it is probably best to stop this exercise (or any other) and seek advice before proceeding. Hyperventilation does involve risks. Pain in your back, thighs, or legs may indicate that you carry considerable tension in those parts of your body. This exercise can help release this tension. But, here, too, my advice is to discontinue any exercise that causes discomfort or pain and seek professional advice.

## *Exercise #5.* Grounding Exercise

Stand with your feet about ten to twelve inches apart, with your toes pointed somewhat towards each other,

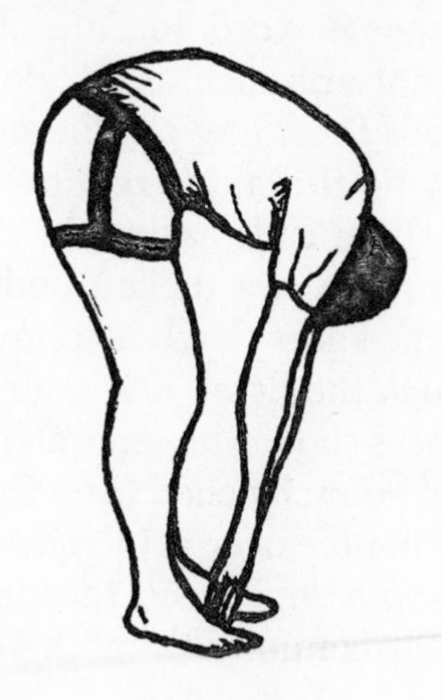

and your knees slightly bent. Touch your fingers to the floor in front of you, bending your knees a little more if necessary. Allow your head to hang loosely. Your hands are positioned properly when they are far enough in front of you so that you need the finger contact with the floor to keep balanced, but not so far forward that your fingers support any of your body weight. Keep your weight on the balls of your feet, with your heels flat on the floor.

Inhale, then make a sound as you exhale as you did in Exercise #4. While breathing in and out, very gradually straighten your knees—but not to the point where they lock—until your legs start vibrating. Then keep your knees in the position at which the vibrations began. Try not to straighten your knees too rapidly, because you may miss the point at which these vibrations start. The vibrations may spread to other parts of your body. When they become involuntary and smooth, the vibrations serve to stimulate and unlock your breathing.

## *Exercise #6. Ki* Breathing

*Ki* is the Japanese word for life energy. Adepts in Japanese martial arts such as Aikido, have developed various methods for filling or charging the body with ki. The following technique requires that you sit in a traditional position called *seiza.* In this Japanese style of sitting, your legs are tucked under you. To sit in seiza, bend your knees slowly and lower yourself until your knees touch the floor. Rest your buttocks on your heels. Your knees should be separated by the width of two or three of your clenched fists. Cross your big toes, with your left big toe over your right big toe. Let your hands rest in your lap. Keep the small of your back straight, and sit comfortably with your shoulders relaxed.

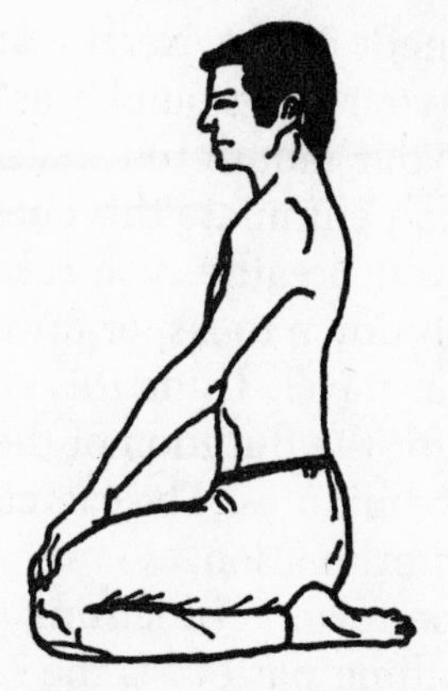

Once you are in position, begin the exercise with the following breathing pattern: Open your mouth and make a "hah!" sound as you exhale slowly and smoothly through your mouth. Direct the air toward a point on the floor about five feet in front of you. Maintain your sitting position as you exhale, until your lungs are almost empty. At that point, keeping your back straight, bend forward slightly to release the rest of the air in your lungs.

At first, your exhalation may last only fifteen to twenty seconds. But in time, you will find that the exhalation will lengthen to thirty to forty seconds without any strain. After completing the exhalation, keep leaning slightly forward, close your mouth, and wait two to three seconds before inhaling.

Now inhale through your nose. Like the out-breath, the in-breath should be slow and smooth. Remain in the slightly forward position until you come to the end of your inhalation. At that point, straighten again to breathe in the last bit of air. As with your exhalation, your inhalation will initially be short, but in time it will last twenty to twenty-five seconds.

Hold your breath for five to ten seconds; then begin another cycle. While holding your breath, you may experience tension, tightness, or strain in your chest. This decreases the benefit of the exercise and can cause the air to rush out of your lungs quickly and uncontrollably when you open your mouth to exhale.

Usually, you can eliminate this chest tension by imagining that as you breathe, you take the air in your lungs and move it down to a spot in your body an inch or two below your navel. Using this visualization, continue breathing for the duration of the exercise, generally five to twenty minutes. The exercise always ends as it starts, with an exhalation.

You can also perform ki breathing while sitting in a chair. Your breathing pattern is the same as described above, but instead of sitting seiza, sit in a chair with your back straight (but not rigid). Do not lean your back against the chair.

You can also perform ki breathing in supine and standing positions. In the supine position, lie on your back with both feet stretched out. Support your head on a pillow. In this posture, modify your basic breathing pattern to eliminate bending the body forward and backward as in the sitting positions. In the standing position, perform ki breathing the same way you did in the sitting positions.

# 9

# Embodied: Caring for Our Bodies

*I learned that the form and the movement of my bodily expression reveal the nature of my existence. I learned that I am my body. My body is me.*

Stanley Keleman

Our body is a major aspect of who we are and hence vital to our developing a strong sense of self-worth. On one extreme, there are narcissists, who find self-identity only in their bodies. On the other extreme, there are ascetics, who reject their bodies completely in an effort to gain self-understanding. Both of these approaches to meaningful living are deeply misguided. As I have said, balance is the key; true self-worth resides at neither extreme.

People who are balanced respect their bodies as part of their totality and act accordingly. They have learned that such respect is enriching in every way. Why? Because our bodies are ultimately the instrument through which we express physically all that we are. Just as an out-of-tune piano will limit the performance of even the most talented pianist, so too a malfunctioning body will hinder our personal development.

When we become physically ill, we feel less joyful about ourselves and our lives. Conversely, when we increase our physical well-being and vitality, we feel more zestful and optimistic about everything. We think more clearly, function more effectively, and have a greater sense of self-direction. When we care for our bodies, we not only avoid diagnosed illnesses, but vitalize our overall involvement in life and increase our self-worth.

Of course, many forces contribute to our physical well-being, some of which are beyond our control. However, we can exert considerable control over many health factors, including diet, exercise, and exposure to sunlight. A deficiency in any of these areas is often important enough to make the difference between health and sickness—between optimal daily functioning and just getting by. This chapter discusses health issues that we can learn to control to achieve greater enjoyment in living.

## YOU ARE WHAT YOU EAT

What we eat and drink has a major impact on our health. This fact is neither recognized nor heeded often enough, even by those intimately concerned with our physical well-being. In the four years I spent there, the medical school I attended did not offer students a single course in nutrition. As recently as the mid-1970s, Dr. Jean Mayer, President of Tufts University pointedly observed:

> We have just completed a study to find out what the average doctor at Harvard knows about nutrition. What we found out is this: the average doctor at Harvard knows a wee bit more about nutrition than his [or her] secretary, unless his [or her] secretary has a

weight problem, in which case the average secretary knows a wee bit more about nutrition than the average doctor.

Fortunately, this situation is now starting to change. But until recently, my training was characteristic of medical school training throughout the United States. The subject of nutrition was addressed by declaring that if people consumed a balanced diet, all of their nutritional needs, including vitamin and mineral requirements would be adequately met. It was more than a decade after I received my M.D. that I came to see that this generally held viewpoint is erroneous. It is actually a cultural myth, like the myth that Americans are "the best-fed people in the world." When we accept such truisms at face value, we endanger both our physical health and our self-worth.

Medical researchers have long known that severe nutritional deficiencies can cause severe mental illness. In recent years, investigators examining less serious mental disorders have found evidence that emotional distress is caused or worsened by poor nutrition. Other investigators have discovered that some people are genetically predisposed to nutritional deficiencies or are affected adversely in subtle ways by particular foods. It is now clear that nutrition plays a vital role in influencing our day-to-day moods and outlook.

Even more significantly, it is now apparent that we are affected by everything we eat. We can no longer afford the dubious luxury of ignoring the link between diet and health. Because of environmental damage, many foods no longer have their former nutritional content. It is a sad and ominous fact that few of us can regularly buy wholesome, organically-grown, non-contaminated food. Contamination of one sort or another now takes place at nearly every step in the process of food growth and preparation.

## INDIVIDUAL DIFFERENCES IN NUTRITION

Given the deficiencies in the foods we can buy, many people now rely on dietary supplements, such as vitamin and mineral tablets. However, the specific combination of supplements each of us needs must be individualized for us to get maximum benefit. Just as the needs for sleep and sexual release vary from person to person and from one life stage to another, so too our nutritional requirements vary. A health professional must consider many factors before recommending an optimal diet for a patient. Usually, the best way to get personalized help is to consult a qualified professional.*

However, some basic nutritional concepts are almost universally applicable. If I were asked to offer a single such rule, I would unhesitatingly suggest: do not overeat! This is the single most important dietary law, and it has been known for centuries. For example, Maimonides, a twelfth-century physician and healer, blamed overeating—even of "good" foods—for many kinds of illness. In our own day, Paavo Airola, naturopathic physician and nutritionist has stated:

> Systematic undereating is the NUMBER ONE health and longevity secret. Overeating, on the other hand,

---

*People interested in referrals to physicians who practice nutritional medicine as described in this chapter should contact: The American College of Advancement in Medicine (ACAM), 23121 Verdugo Drive, Laguna Hills, California 92653. Phone (714) 583-7666, or (800) 532-3688.

A list of physicians who evaluate and treat patients for food sensitivities, as discussed in this chapter, can be obtained from The American Academy of Environmental Medicine, P.O. Box 16106, Denver, Colorado 80216. Phone (303) 622-9755. Many physicians are members of both organizations.

> *even of health foods*, is one of the main causes of disease and premature aging. . . . Overeating is especially dangerous for older people, who are less active and have a slowed down metabolism. (p. 199)

It is also crucial that we pay attention to how and when we eat. Our overall health is best served when we eat in a relaxed setting, without rushing. A relaxed atmosphere improves the digestion and assimilation of our food. Eating under conditions that cause tension undermines our self-worth both physiologically and psychologically. In fact, eating under tense conditions is an expression of how little we value ourselves and how much we value instead the dictates of others. It is usually better to skip a meal than to eat under pressure. If we are so rushed that the only way we can eat is on the run or in an unpleasant environment, we obviously lack respect for our body, and this lack inevitably damages our self-worth. To change our lifestyle, we must reorder our priorities.

There are two general guidelines regarding when to eat: First, eat only when you are hungry. If you eat for any other reason, you are disregarding your body's wisdom and diminishing its voice. Eat slowly and chew each bite very well. Doing so contributes to good digestion and gives us greater satisfaction with less food. Unfortunately, we often begin ignoring our body's signals about hunger or fullness during infancy, when many of us are fed according to an external schedule rather than according to our inner rhythms. As children get older, they are confronted with messages that further confuse their inner signals. Haven't we all been told: "How can you be hungry? You just ate a little while ago." Or, "Don't eat now; we're going to have dinner soon!" Or, "You can't leave the dinner table until you finish everything on your plate!"

Second, it is better to eat several small meals spaced throughout the day than to eat two or three large meals. Interestingly, the same number of calories consumed during several small meals will cause less weight gain than the same number of calories ingested in one or two large meals. Regarding what to eat and what to avoid, the advice of nutrition experts conflicts sharply. Indeed, if you follow the dietary prohibitions set down by each school of thought, you will find almost nothing acceptable to eat. However, there seems to be a general consensus among nutritionists that it is important to eat whole unprocessed foods, and that a significant portion of this food should be in its raw, whole state, including seeds, nuts, fruits, and most vegetables.

Nevertheless, each person's optimal diet is likely to be different, because of genetic differences and unsuspected food sensitivities. A food sensitivity has features of both an allergy and an addiction. Eating a food to which we are sensitive can cause a wide variety of symptoms, such as fatigue, lethargy, depression, anxiety, headaches, rapid weight gain, indigestion, and even seizures and hallucinations. These symptoms can affect any part of our bodies.

Most people are familiar with the idea of food allergies. People who are allergic to a specific food—for instance, strawberries—will break out in a rash or hives if they eat that food. Similarly, it is well known that some asthmatics experience difficulty in breathing caused by a constriction of lung tissue when they are exposed to a food or other substance to which they are allergic.

Our sinuses are also often affected by allergies, as is commonly seen in hay fever, an allergy to pollen. When hay fever sufferers come into contact with pollen, their sinuses react, though their skin usually remains unaffected. However, allergy induced asthma attacks generally do not involve either the sinuses or skin. Similarly, the hives we get from a skin allergy typically do not affect our lungs or sinuses. Thus, when the body is exposed to a sensitizing agent, it responds selectively: one part responds while others continue to function normally. Moreover, medical evidence suggests that every organ of the body, not just the skin, lungs, and sinuses, can manifest symptoms when it is exposed to a substance, whether food or chemical, to which it is sensitive.*

Food sensitivity reactions, therefore, can occur in any part of the body in response to eating a particular food, no matter how wholesome it is. A food sensitivity differs from a food allergy not only in that a sensitivity can cause a broader range of symptoms, but also in that some food sensitivities may affect the body through a mechanism other than the antigen-antibody formation characteristic of allergies. In addition, allergies are generally fixed responses. Once they become established, they continue indefinitely. However, food sensitivities are considerably more fickle. They often dissipate if we avoid the offending food for a few months. In those people who are predisposed, however, new sensitivities can develop continually.

Food sensitivities also have features of an addiction, in that sufferers tend to get "hooked" on the foods to which they are sensitive. If we have food sensitivities, we often crave exactly those foods to which we are sensitive, eat them regularly, and even describe them as our favorites. We may experience withdrawal when we do not eat these foods for a while, and sometimes feel that we can overcome symptoms such as fatigue or listlessness by eating the food. Thus, ironically, we

---

*For more information on the ideas presented in this chapter, see David Sheinkin, Michael Schachter, and Richard Hutton, *Food, Mind and Mood* (New York, 1987).

may repeatedly consume the very substances which are undermining our health.

Think of the people who munch chocolate or candy bars throughout the day to keep themselves going. Or those who make similar use of coffee or cigarettes, to counteract their recurring periods of fatigue, which are in fact a withdrawal symptom. Since eating the sensitizing food stops an unpleasant sensation such as fatigue, it is easy for afflicted individuals to view the sensitizing food as something that makes them feel better, even though it actually has a negative effect on the body. Since sensitivity symptoms can be induced by any food, food additive, or supplement, the health of many people is compromised by reactions to foods to which they have an unknown and unsuspected sensitivity.

The existence of food sensitivities can easily be demonstrated scientifically. Yet, food sensitivity is a relatively new concept—only about forty years old. In medical history, most ideas must be around longer than this before they gain widespread acceptance. As a result, most people, including many physicians, are not yet familiar with the concept of food sensitivity, and therefore, improperly diagnose or dismiss many symptoms caused by it. Some people do not even recognize their symptoms as physical reactions ("That's just the way I am"), or mistakenly attribute them to other factors ("What do you expect with the kind of pressure I work under?"). When we cannot recognize or accept symptoms like fatigue as problems we can overcome, we reduce our ability to enhance our vitality.

However, it is not always simple to determine accurately the presence of food sensitivities. Indeed, because of certain complicating factors, it is frequently impossible to base this determination solely on an analysis of our diet. The most reliable method of determining food sensitivities is to eliminate most or all of the suspected food allergens by following an elimination diet for four days to a week to see if our symptoms improve. If improvement occurs, then we can add suspected foods to our diet one at a time, while checking for reactions. It is a good idea to check with a physician or other health care practitioner before starting an elimination diet. Other methods of testing include blood tests which measure antibodies to specific foods either directly or indirectly.

We can also perform a subjective test for food sensitivities at home. Though the test presently lacks full scientific acceptance, it is clinically useful. Developed by Dr. George Goodheart, founder of the medical field known as applied kinesiology, the test involves determining the strength of a muscle before and after the food to be tested is placed under the subject's tongue. A weakness of the muscle after the food has been placed under the tongue suggests a sensitivity to that food. Instructions on how to perform this test are in the exercises at the end of this chapter.

Although people familiar with the concept of chi have no trouble understanding or accepting this method of testing, it is baffling to mainstream health care practitioners. Yet, we know that material in contact with our tongues can be absorbed into the body very rapidly. For instance, persons suffering from angina pectoris (heart pain resulting from decreased blood circulation) are often advised to place a nitroglycerine tablet under their tongues to relax their coronary arteries. This method of administering the drug aids in its rapid absorption and offers prompt relief.

We also know that all matter is composed of atoms, which are in turn composed of electrical particles in rapid motion. Thus, all matter can be viewed as a manifestation of radiating fields of energy. Whether applied kinesiology is based on the concept of chi, the interaction of energy fields, a neurolingual reflex, or a yet undiscovered factor, it does provide us with valuable information regarding our health and well-being.

When an applied kinesiology testing reveals that a specific food is a major sensitizing agent, the affected person should discontinue eating the food for six to twelve weeks. Usually within a week of eliminating the food, symptoms will start to disappear. In some cases, testing will reveal that a person is sensitive to so many foods that eliminating them all would be impractical. In this case, it is best to consult a physician trained in this field.

Besides eliminating specific foods to which sensitivities exist, we would do well to evaluate our daily diet as a whole if we want to achieve optimal well-being. We should especially avoid "junk foods" as much as possible. In this category are foods that are highly processed, contain hydrogenated fats or sugar as a major ingredient, or include artificial additives. We should also avoid common drugs such as alcohol, nicotine, and caffeine.

## PHYSICAL EXERCISE

Factors other than diet also are essential in helping us live a vital life. Without physical exercise, for example, we cannot properly digest or metabolize food. In this regard, I agree with Dr. Airola's statement, "It is better to eat junk foods and exercise a lot, than to eat health foods and not exercise at all."

Like diet, proper exercise in our society is all too often accorded only lip service. As a physician, I hear countless excuses for not exercising regularly. Perhaps the most common is "I'd like to, but I don't have the time." Other people say, "It's boring!"; "I don't like to exercise alone"; "I'm not disciplined enough"; or "I don't know which exercises to do."

All of these statements are really ways of saying, "I don't value myself enough." Here again, our basic lack of respect for our bodies, coupled with the adverse physiological effects of insufficient exercise, will limit the development of self-worth. Can we truly lack the time to nurture our own health?

We can engage in adequate exercise either indoors or outdoors without elaborate and expensive equipment. Some types of exercise are relatively unstructured, such as jogging, bicycle riding, and swimming. Others require more practice, such as yoga, tennis, and psychocalisthenics. There are many good books on exercise that can get you started on an exercise program.

Like diet, physical exercise often needs to be individualized. A doctor must consider many factors to determine the type, length, and frequency of exercise that can help a person achieve optimal well-being. We can certainly experiment with various exercise programs on our own. Nevertheless, it is often useful to seek the advice of someone knowledgeable, such as a physician, before embarking on a strenuous exercise regimen.

### SUNLIGHT AND HEALTH

Unlike our needs for good nutrition and adequate physical exercise, our need for sunlight is medically recognized much less often. However, this situation too has changed dramatically in recent years. Of course, the best-known benefit of sunlight is its role in producing Vitamin D in the body. Though scientists generally recognize that sunlight exerts a profound effect on plant life, they are only beginning to learn of its equally profound effect on animals.

One of the leading figures in this field is John Ott. In his book *Health and Light,* Ott recounted how his initial awareness of light's healthful effects developed from his work with time-lapse photography. He discovered that by varying the color or wavelength of light to which certain plants were exposed, he could control the gender of the flowers produced by those plants.

In 1970 research showed that such effects are not limited to plants. Two thousand chinchilla ranchers around the world participated in a study which concluded that the type of lighting used in chinchilla breeding rooms greatly influenced the gender of newborn animals. Specifically, incandescent light produced litters that were largely male; "daylight" incandescent bulbs yielded litters that were mostly female. Scientists also found that it was not the breeding room's temperature, but the light's periodicity that affected the growth of heavy fur on chinchillas.

In the same year, another published study showed that the number and severity of dental cavities in hamsters were dependent on the amount of natural versus simulated sunlight to which they were exposed. A group of hamsters was fed a diet high in carbohydrates. Half of the animals were exposed to light from standard fluorescent tubes. They developed an average of eleven cavities. However, animals exposed to fluorescent tubes with added ultraviolet light—simulating sunlight—averaged only about two cavities, despite eating the same diet.

The poultry industry has long capitalized on the knowledge that the light entering chickens' eyes stimulates their pituitary glands and increases egg production. Many animal studies now support the idea that the mammalian hormonal system responds to particular wavelengths of visible light, ultraviolet light, and other areas of the total light spectrum.

Scientific research has also demonstrated that proper functioning of our endocrine system depends on exposure to the full spectrum of light. Many studies document diseases that were precipitated or aggravated by lack of sunlight, and later cured or ameliorated when the subject was exposed to an appropriate amount of sunlight. A pilot investigation conducted by the National Institute of Mental Health demonstrated that certain forms of depression, now called seasonal affective disorder (SAD), can be alleviated or cured through exposure to bright light. Subsequent research has confirmed that sunlight deprivation induces winter depression in some individuals. Exposure to the sun's ultraviolet radiation has also been found to lower blood pressure and levels of cholesterol in the blood.

Scientific findings indicate too that for the best health, we need to be exposed to the full spectrum of sunlight. When parts of this spectrum, particularly ultraviolet light, are filtered out, our emotional as well as our physical health can be adversely affected. However, getting adequate exposure to sunlight is not always easy in our urban society. Ordinary glass prevents ninety-seven percent of the sun's ultraviolet light from passing through. Therefore, if our exposure to the sun is only through glass like an office window or a car windshield, we are not experiencing the full spectrum of light. Similarly, eyeglasses and sunglasses block ultraviolet light from reaching our retinas. Most artificial sources of light are gross distortions of the visible light spectrum and are almost totally devoid of ultraviolet light.

Making matters worse for us, polluted air disturbs our light supply, quite apart from its other detrimental effects on our health. The Smithsonian Institute in Washington, D.C., has reported that during the last fifty years the overall intensity of light reaching Americans has decreased 14 percent. Even at higher elevations, such as at the observatory on Mt. Wilson, there are reports that during the same period, there has been a 10 percent decrease in the average intensity of sunlight, and a 26 percent decrease in the ultraviolet part of the spectrum.

Such information is particularly important for those of us who spend most of our daylight hours indoors. The obvious remedy would be for us to spend as much time as possible outdoors without lenses. If this arrangement is impractical, the next best thing would be for us to use *full spectrum* indoor lighting.

By this I mean, we should install fluorescent bulbs that produce light more like natural sunlight. Ott and others have been instrumental in persuading manufacturers to produce these bulbs. Since full spectrum bulbs fit standard fluorescent fixtures, it is easy and inexpensive to use them in place of regular bulbs. Undoubtedly, as we acquire more knowledge about the overall health effects of full spectrum sunlight, even better lighting materials and lenses will be available.

However, before we dash out into the sunshine, it is important to be aware of its hazards. Like all good things in life, it is possible to get too much sun. Overexposure to sunlight and sunburning, especially repetitive burning over many years, damages the skin irreparably. Chronic intense exposure to ultraviolet radiation causes the skin's fibers to lose their stretchiness and resiliency so that the suppleness of youthful skin fades away. Melanocytes, the pigment-producing cells in the skin, can become damaged causing patchy brown spots to appear, surrounded by unpigmented areas. After many years of overexposure, even the glands that secrete lubricants lose their efficiency. Eventually, our skin becomes dried, sagging, and wrinkled.

Far more serious than this cosmetic problem is the link between ultraviolet radiation and skin cancer. Each year, hundreds of thousands of new cases of skin cancer are diagnosed in the United States. Epidemiologists believe that this increase reflects the popularity of sunbathing in the early 1960s. Skin malignancies are more prevalent in tropical and subtropical latitudes. Fortunately, many skin cancers are at least partially preventable, and over 90 percent are curable if treatment begins soon enough.*

Interest in light and health is clearly increasing. In 1984, the New York Academy of Sciences hosted the first international conference on the medical and biological effects of light. As evidenced by the wide range of topics covered, it seems that the scientific community is now confirming what many world cultures have long taught, that besides being a potentially dangerous force, sunlight is a primordial, necessary element of life.

## EXERCISES FOR TESTING SUBSTANCE SENSITIVITIES

The following exercises, all requiring the aid of a partner, enable you to determine sensitivity to foods and other substances. These methods are routinely used in Applied Kinesiology, discussed earlier in this chapter. Admittedly, they are the least scientifically proven of

*Since Dr. Sheinkin wrote this chapter, the danger of sunlight to our skin has increased due to the partial destruction of our earth's ozone layer.

the pertinent diagnostic tests currently available. Besides their current lack of statistical validation, these exercises can be faulted for their clearly subjective nature. That is, you or your partner can influence the outcome by varying the pressure from one trial to the next.

Nevertheless, applied kinesiology's results appear to be helpful empirically during clinical trials. Hence, a growing number of physicians, chiropractors, and other health care practitioners are utilizing kinesiology in therapeutic work. If you are willing to be open-minded, your own experience with these tests may persuade you of their validity.

## *Exercise #1.* Food Sensitivity Test

STEP 1. Prepare samples of a food that you wish to test. A small amount of each food—one or two bites—is usually sufficient.

STEP 2. Next, have your partner test your initial muscle strength. For example, for your partner to test your left arm, extend it straight out sideways while you face your partner. Your partner places his or her left hand on your right shoulder for stabilization. Your partner then places either the whole right hand or a few fingers of the right hand on your left wrist and then tries to force your arm down by slowly applying increasing downward pressure.

Using muscle power, do your best to resist the downward push. But remember, this is not an arm-wrestling contest; the two of you are not competing against one another, but cooperating to determine your arm's baseline strength or resistance. That is, you are jointly gauging the least amount of force needed to push your arm down. Whether your partner requires a single finger, one hand, or two hands to push your wrist down indicates the relative difference in strength between the two of you.

A variation of this procedure involves placing the tips of your thumb and forefinger together and forming a ring. While you press your fingers hard together to keep the ring intact, your partner places a finger of each hand inside the ring (one finger against your thumb and one finger against your forefinger) and tries to pull your ring apart. In this case, the same cooperative attitude and gradual increase in pressure is necessary to obtain a valid measure of your baseline strength.

STEP 3. Allow time, if necessary, for the tested muscles to relax. When you feel rested, go on to the next step.

STEP 4. Place a small amount of the food being tested in your mouth. If it is solid, chew it thoroughly. If it is liquid, hold it in your mouth. In either case, do not swallow it. The test is conducted with the food in your mouth, preferably touching your tongue and mixing with your saliva.

After you have retained the food in your mouth for about thirty seconds, have your partner retest the muscle as in Step 2. If you have a sensitivity to the food, your muscle will now be considerably weaker. If you have no sensitivity to the food, your muscle strength will remain unchanged. In some cases, when the item contains nutrients that you currently lack, you may experience a surprising increase in muscular strength.

If you encounter weakness, remove the food from your mouth. If necessary, rinse your mouth, and your strength will return. Each time you replace the food in your mouth, your muscle will feel weaker again.

You can test a variety of foods, one after another or in combination. Sometimes, a combination can cause weakness even though individual foods do not. In each case, remember not to swallow the food, but rather perform the test while the food is in your mouth, mixed with saliva, and touching your tongue. If you encounter a food that weakens your muscles, rinse your mouth thoroughly before testing the next item.

## *Exercise #2.* Food Supplement Sensitivity Test

Food supplements such as vitamins and mineral preparations, as well as medications, can also cause sensitivity reactions. These can be tested in a similar manner to Exercise #1.

Place the tablet or capsule under your tongue after wetting it with your saliva. Keep it there for about thirty seconds and perform the steps indicated above.

Sometimes, you may be sensitive to the capsule itself but not to its contents. Similarly, if the tablet is coated, you can test the contents with, and then without, the coating. Usually it can be removed by holding the tablet under running water and rubbing the coating off.

## *Exercise #3.* Household Chemical Sensitivity Test

Chemicals also frequently cause sensitivity symptoms. On an everyday basis, most of us come into contact with hundreds if not thousands of synthetic chemicals. These exist in many soaps, toothpastes, hair sprays, perfumes, shaving creams and lotions, deodorants, and in permanent press clothing, carpeting, and plastic items.

The method for testing synthetic chemicals is essentially the same as that described for foods. The exception is that you inhale them, instead of putting them into your mouth. Obviously, do not use this procedure to test chemicals that are dangerous to inhale.*

*This chapter was reviewed and, where necessary, updated by Michael B. Schachter, M.D.

# 10

# Personal Mystery Lessons

*Every journey has a secret destination of which the traveler is unaware.*

Martin Buber

In our increasingly fragmented society, we are all influenced by what can be called a "victim mentality." With this limited and limiting perspective, we typically go through our days blaming others when things do not go exactly our way. In extreme cases, we may become so habituated to feeling victimized through one situation after another that our creative capabilities are almost wholly immobilized. In my therapeutic work, I see patients all the time who are stuck blaming someone or some situation for their lack of inner harmony. Of course, this kind of thinking is not found only in psychiatric consultation rooms.

Do we have an alternative to the victim outlook? In this chapter, I offer a distinctly different, more empowering way of regarding our lives. It is based on accepting a few fundamental assumptions that have been espoused by the world's great spiritual teachers for millennia. Around the globe, these axioms have proven over and over to be attitudes that significantly enhance a sense of meaning and self-worth.

Despite their effectiveness, I do not insist that these assumptions are literally true. They are clearly beyond rational proof and therefore not scientifically verifiable. But as American philosopher William James insisted at the turn of the century, philosophical beliefs that enrich us practically should always be taken seriously. As founder of the intellectual school known as pragmatism, James argued in his *Varieties of Religious Experience* that mystical teachings can be very useful in our everyday lives. If we allow ourselves to take an "as if" approach, and let these key assumptions guide us for even a few days, we will swiftly see their empowering effects.

The first assumption is that *nothing happens by coincidence*. This notion differs markedly from the view held by many in our society that we live in a universe ruled by blind chance and sheer randomness.

The second assumption is that *everything happens for a positive purpose*. That purpose may not always be readily apparent, but as we grow in wisdom and discernment, we are far more likely to perceive that everything happens for the good.

Third, we assume that *each of us is born on earth to learn specific lessons*.

These three related assumptions provide us with a picture of the cosmos far more uplifting than the worldview offered by the dominant culture, with its corresponding unprovable axioms, which are much darker in their view of human existence.

## UNIVERSAL TEACHINGS

It is striking that mystical traditions from different cultures and historical periods all preach the same fundamental truths about the human condition. Such divergent spiritual systems as Hinduism, Kabbalah, Native American shamanism, Sufism, Tibetan Buddhism, and esoteric Christianity all teach that we come to earth much as a child goes to school. That is, though the particular religious symbolism varies, these systems commonly stress that earthly existence resembles an educational facility in which we all are enrolled.

In this school, we must all take basic courses, corresponding to reading, social studies, science, writing, arithmetic and other skills, in order to graduate. Our spiritual lessons may encompass learning to love and trust; to develop compassion, empathy, kindness, and humility; to accept responsibility for our actions; and other related lessons with which we each struggle daily. In the long run, we all have the same courses to take, because the overall curriculum to be fully human is unchanging. But at any given moment, we are each working on different aspects of this universal course of study.

You may have already mastered a particular course that I have yet to begin—perhaps, how to act more compassionately towards people who are suffering. I may be in the midst of a course that you have just started, for example, how to have proper self-discipline. Life presents us with countless opportunities to learn our lessons.

A related concept that can guide our everyday lives is the existence of a higher aspect to our being, of which we are typically completely unaware. Of course, Sigmund Freud's great contribution to our age was the concept that our conscious mind is like the tip of an iceberg—the part that rises above the water may look like a mountain, but it is actually only a small portion of the entire mass. Freud and his colleagues at the turn of this century effectively demonstrated that our minds include an active force of which the conscious part of our minds may be wholly oblivious. Freud's realization has influenced our entire culture. For example, look at the billions of dollars spent each year on advertising designed to affect us unconsciously.

But long before Freud, the world's great mystics talked about the human unconscious. Interestingly, they not only spoke of what Freud broadly identified, but they also explicitly recognized a *higher* unconscious within us. The various spiritual systems have expressed it differently, but we will call it the "superconscious." It influences us perhaps even more powerfully than the part of our mind below our familiar awareness.

How does Freud's subconscious differ from the superconscious? For one thing, that which lies *below* our consciousness is very personal, including our desires, thoughts, and memories. In contrast, the superconscious is a more universal consciousness—it is in touch with everything. Thus, my superconsciousness may be attuned to your superconsciousness, even though consciously we may not suspect that anything at all is occurring between us.

This notion may explain psychic phenomena like telepathy. Perhaps, telepathy is actually a form of communication from one superconsciousness to another. But more concretely, just as Freudian analysts insist that we can understand our subconscious, mystics have taught that we can understand the superconscious. How? Through the practice of meditation, which I have already discussed in this book. Meditating helps to expand our awareness of our superconscious. But as important as meditation is, it is secondary to attitudinal empowerment. When we stop seeing ourselves as victims, but see ourselves instead as active agents and collaborators in life's situations, we experience greater satisfaction and meaning in living.

Esoteric traditions also share the view that we are often presented in life with what might be called "mystery lessons." These are experiences that seem unpleasant, but are vital to our inner development. They are a mystery because we are conditioned to expect growth to be fun or satisfying, and negative events to be accidental and meaningless. But mystics emphasize that dealing with "mystery lessons" is a key avenue toward self-growth, and ultimately, toward enhancing self-worth.

Finally, all spiritual traditions teach that if we see the meaning of a particular lesson clearly and learn it successfully, we will probably never have to learn it again in exactly the same way. A mystery lesson, consequently, is a part of our earthly curriculum in which we are presented with a situation that we have not yet handled well. It is not that our Higher Teacher—ultimately, God—is angry at us or is trying to hurt us. Rather, a seemingly negative situation is in fact a potential tool we can use to further our own self-realization.

How can we recognize a mystery lesson when it occurs? There are two main criteria, either of which may apply in a particular situation. When both criteria apply simultaneously, we can be reasonably certain that we are dealing with a true mystery lesson.

The first criterion is that the situation is repetitive. If we find ourselves in a state of affairs that keeps recurring, we should probably view it as a mystery lesson. Why? Because the fact that something is repetitive indicates that we have not dealt with it. The subject matter can be insignificant, or it can affect our entire life. Initially, the lesson may come lightly, even in a dream; but if we don't learn the lesson, it will recur in forms harder and harder to ignore. This escalation is not a stern or unjust form of punishment, but rather an increasingly urgent message meant to call our attention to the lesson plan. Nearly all of us have at times experienced recurrent patterns, such as having one unsatisfying job or unhappy relationship after another, each troubled by the same type of difficulty. If so, we are probably being presented with a mystery lesson.

The second criterion is that the negative situation makes us especially vulnerable or reactive. The tip-off is that we notice ourselves becoming unusually angry, frustrated, fearful, apathetic, or otherwise negatively charged. In such instances, we are being given a mystery lesson meant to stimulate our personal development.

Thus, if we find ourselves in a repetitive, unpleasant situation that arouses intense negative feeling in us, we are almost certainly in the midst of a mystery lesson.

## UNRAVELING A PERSONAL MYSTERY LESSON

Several years ago, I was involved with a group of about a dozen physicians and nurses who were studying with a healer. Because the group's members lived all over the New York metropolitan area, we met at a different site each week. On one particular Sunday, I was hosting the group at my house. During the previous few sessions, my colleagues and I had become particularly close, and I was excited about being host that day.

During the same months, my wife Lynn was attending graduate school at Columbia University. I knew that on the afternoon of my meeting, she would need to do reserve reading at the Columbia library. At that time we had three children. A day or two before my study group meeting, I asked her, "What about the kids? Who'll watch them?"

Smiling, Lynn replied, "It's all taken care of. I've made arrangements for them to go to their friends' houses."

I was relieved and pleased. I would have the whole house to myself and my group without any interruptions. When Sunday morning arrived, I was in a mood of happy anticipation. But as the hours passed, I noticed uneasily that only two of my children were eating breakfast, and bustling around the house getting dressed. My youngest, Ari, still had pajamas on. Meanwhile, my wife was gathering her college books and obviously getting ready to leave.

Uneasily, I said to Lynn, "Ari still isn't dressed."

"Yes, we've had a change in plans," Lynn replied tensely. "He can't go to his friend's house. He's coming with me."

This struck me as a terrible idea. How could she do library research with him underfoot? But I decided to say nothing. I did not want Ari around my study group, either. Another half hour passed, and Ari was still in pajamas. My wife was now about to leave the house with our other two children. As calmly as I could, I said to Lynn, "Ari is still not dressed."

She replied hastily, "He's sick, and now he has a rever. He can't go out at all. He has to stay in. You'll have to check on him every hour. Make sure he gets his vitamins and fluids. Be sure he stays warm."

As she continued to list the things I was supposed to do, I began to get angry. Her voice began to rise too as she stepped out the door and turned toward me. Each additional task that she enumerated felt like a knife twisting in me. Suddenly I became furious and started shouting at her in the driveway.

Lynn got into the car and yelled back at me, "This is finals week! I have to go to the library today. The books are all on reserve, so I can't stay home with Ari.

You're his father, right? You'll be home all day, anyway."

I was equally adamant, "You know this is my last class. All my colleagues will be coming over expecting a relaxed meeting! How can I host the session with Ari needing constant care and attention?"

We each had our point, but the argument was ended abruptly by the screeching sound of the car pulling out of the driveway. I was so enraged that I felt like grabbing the vehicle. Going back into the house, I saw that the den where I planned to have the meeting was a complete mess. Books and papers were strewn everywhere. I knew I had enough time to tidy up, but I was too angry to do it. I was stewing with anger and just wanted to dash after Lynn's car to bring her back.

Then I said to myself, "This is no good. I've got to get myself composed before people start to arrive."

I sat down on the floor, began my relaxation exercises and meditation, and really worked on calming myself. When I finally succeeded, I knew I had a big problem. When my wife got home that evening, we were going to have a huge fight. But I hoped that I would be calm at least through the afternoon. I rose from my meditation, and began straightening the books and papers strewn around the house.

At that moment, the telephone rang. It was my answering service. "I have an emergency for you," said the operator. "It's from your patient Mrs. Gates."

"Who?"

I asked that the name be repeated, and then repeated again. I had never heard of a Mrs. Gates. My answering service operator insisted that Mrs. Gates had just called, urgently asking that I provide specific medical information about her condition. At that moment, I experienced a strange feeling of déjà vu.

I must have paused for a long time, for the operator

nearly barked, "Are you hearing me? Mrs. Gates says that it's urgent. You have to call her right now!"

Still smouldering over the earlier scene, I became furious again. I felt like throttling the operator as I slammed down the receiver, my hand shaking. Once more I began pacing the living room.

Suddenly, I realized that I had become extremely angry twice within the last half hour. I said to myself, "If this is a mystery lesson, then I'm going to have to deal with it."

I sat down to think, and within seconds, I understood my lesson. My anger and tension dissipated.

What was the subject being taught? The great spiritual traditions agree that such lessons are rarely pleasant, and I now saw clearly that mine was that I was being a hypocrite. How so? I was demanding a day off, free from all responsibility, so that I could learn to become a better healer. Now my own son was sick, but had I wanted to heal him? Not at all. Had I even wanted to be with him? Not in the slightest. Why not? Because I had wanted to learn to become a better healer. Then, I had gotten a phone call from a total stranger who was sick. She wanted healing advice, and I hadn't even wanted to speak with her for two minutes on the telephone. Why not? Because I wanted to learn to become a better healer.

I saw that I had a choice to make. Nobody was forcing me to embark on spiritual healing as part of my practice as a physician. I could have said, "No thank you. I don't want to study techniques of spiritual healing at present." But I said instead, "I want this knowledge; I want to know how to better help suffering people." I saw now that I had to accept the responsibility that comes with such knowledge. And if I did, I simply could not say, "I only want the responsibility of healing others when it's convenient for me."

My higher self was trying to teach me something about the nature of healing. I could almost hear its message aloud: "If you want to become a healer, you must accept a certain amount of responsibility. It takes willingness to do these things. If you are willing to be responsible, you can pursue your quest."

I realized that if I continued to act like an angry victim, what had occurred during the morning would keep recurring—not because God was trying to punish me, but because such events were the nature of earthly existence. I saw, too, that if I planned to become a real healer, more people would be needing and calling me, not necessarily at my convenience. If I could not live comfortably with this situation, if it made me angry and frustrated, and possibly even induced stress-related illness, then I had better not pursue work as a spiritual healer.

Mrs. Gates had not called to anger me. My young son was not sick to anger me. My anger was self-generated, because I was stuck in a hypocritical situation, and I had to make a decision: either abandon my goal of becoming a master healer, or accept responsibility and stop relating to others as if they were imposing on me.

As a result of this attitudinal transformation, I felt much calmer and more self-directed. What happened during my meeting? Our group did not meet in the den, because I never tidied it up. Instead, we met in the living room, which was closer to Ari's bedroom. Every hour, I got up and checked on his condition. I enjoyed the class, and nobody else seemed bothered by the situation at all. The day turned out very well indeed.

But suppose I had maintained my "angry victim" attitude. Most likely, I would have felt certain that every time I left for Ari's bedroom, the group had discussed some crucial topic or shared vital information. I would have rushed back anxiously, demanding to know, "What did so-and-so say? What did I just miss?" When I was caring for my son, I would have been resentful and irritable about even having to get him a glass of water.

But once I understood what my day's mystery lesson was about, I was able to tell myself, "Everyone in the living room is trying to learn about healing. Here, with my son in his room, I'm learning the same thing." Every time I returned to the group, I felt content. I did not feel that I was missing important material. My day became more and more enjoyable. By the time Lynn came home from the library, I had no interest in fighting with her. I simply said, "Thank you. What happened this morning was really wonderful."

Of course, she had no idea what I was talking about, but my attitude was obviously different. My resentment and anger had vanished—or been transformed.

## We Are All Linked

Presumably, if I had not learned my lesson that particular Sunday morning, I would have experienced many similarly frustrating telephone calls and family problems. I needed to learn and accept that being a healer involves responsibility and commitment, that opportunities to practice will not come only at my convenience. I was not a victim but a student learning a valuable lesson. For that I felt grateful and empowered.

What about my wife's role in all this? Am I suggesting that she acted in this case only as a tutor or servant to help me learn my lesson? Of course not. She has her own lessons in life to learn, and I am present in our marriage to help her. The same principle holds true for each of our children. In every family, members are linked spiritually to foster their individual spiritual development. In this sense, we are all teachers to one another, children and parents as much as husband and wife.

Why was my son Ari sick on that particular Sunday? I had not focused attention on that question, because I was trying to learn the responsibility involved in becoming a true healer. But many esoteric traditions teach that illness itself can be a mystery lesson, teaching us something we have failed to learn in a simpler or gentler way. For instance, when a person develops an ulcer, the condition may represent a long ignored lesson about needing to deal more appropriately with anger. Similarly, if someone breaks a toe hurrying around the house, the injury may be a way of saying, "Slow down! Think and plan things more carefully!"

As I mentioned earlier, the great mystical traditions emphasize that everything, even illness, happens for a positive purpose. For instance, the eighteenth-century Kabbalist Rabbi Moses Chaim Luzzatto explained in *The Way of God* that every individual has a challenge, an assignment, and a responsibility in the world. Within this framework, he or she must strive for success. In other words, each person has a particular assignment, so that between them all, everything necessary is accomplished. Moreover, Luzzatto continued, every element is interconnected with every other one in the structure of creation as a whole. And what determined this structure? For Luzzatto and other mystics, "The Highest Wisdom had arranged things in the best and fairest manner." (p. 51)

Or, to offer a contemporary metaphor, imagine a cosmic computer that contains information about us all in its programs. It knows what lessons we each need to learn. So, from on high, a situation was created involving Ari, my wife, and me—and perhaps even Mrs. Gates—so that we all might grow towards our full potential.

When we view events from the unique vantage point of these three assumptions, we can achieve greater harmony in our lives. We no longer feel like helpless victims, but rather like important beings traveling on a divine path for our own benefit. We stop blaming others so readily for our difficulties. Indeed, we no longer think in terms of problems but rather in terms of challenges. We have been presented with an opportunity for inner development.

I can offer another personal example. A few years ago, I spent ten days at a spiritual retreat center in the Southwest. My experience was very stimulating; I felt uplifted and filled with new insights about human existence. After flying back to New York, I met my older son Stephen and my wife at the airport for lunch. When we were sitting in the restaurant, I excitedly began relating my experiences at the retreat. But Stephen interrupted, "Hey, look at the weird guy over there! What's he doing?"

I continued with my narrative, but Stephen soon made an equally distracting comment. It seemed to me that every time I started to relate an interesting experience from my retreat, he interrupted my account.

Just as I was about to lose my temper, I had a flash of insight: could this be a mystery lesson unfolding before me? If so, what was being taught? It was actually fairly easy to explain. I had not seen my son for ten days, and yet I was completely immersed in my own experiences. Since arriving at the restaurant, I had shown almost no interest in him. As a teenager, Stephen had little comprehension of my spiritual interests. In his own way, he was trying to draw attention to the fact that I was ignoring him.

The instant I made this realization, I turned to Stephen and began paying attention to him. I asked questions about his newly acquired skill in skateboarding and the hockey game his underdog team had triumphantly won. We all laughed as he described a clever goal he had scored. Our meal suddenly became quite enjoyable, and everyone was happy. When we got home, Lynn said to me, "You know, what you did at the restaurant impressed me more than anything you could have said about your spiritual retreat."

What had I really done? I had decided to adopt the axiom that everything happens for a purpose as my guide. Stephen's disinterest in my monologue could teach me a specific lesson. Once I saw our interaction from this perspective, I felt empowered and simultaneously closer to my family members.

So our day-to-day lives can be filled with mystery lessons. Whenever we start to feel negative about something, we can look at the situation as a potential lesson, particularly if the situation is recurring. If we embrace this attitude, we can grow considerably in the process.

Such growth brings us toward a new way of seeing ourselves and those around us. It can especially help us become accustomed to the idea that we are not victims, that we attract to ourselves those events and life experiences that we need in order to learn certain lessons. All experiences teach us things, and therefore, all contribute to our spiritual growth. Nothing happens by coincidence.

Is this notion objectively true? Perhaps it is, perhaps not. Perhaps the answer to this question is inherently unknowable. The mystical perspective is certainly quite different from our secular society's customary attitude toward life. It may take a while, therefore, for a true attitudinal change to take place. But I am convinced that if we act *as if* the assumption were true, we immeasurably enrich ourselves, and impart meaning and structure to our lives.

Whenever we find ourselves in a seemingly unpleasant situation, we should ponder, "What is the meaning of this lesson? What do I need to be learning?" Remember, we all have major lessons and minor ones as we go through life. If we start looking at relatively insignificant situations from this perspective, it will become much easier to understand the larger situations. Specific meditative techniques can provide help with mystery lessons, but my purpose here is simply to suggest that if we adopt the attitude that life is our teacher, we will live our days differently and with greater harmony.

## HIDDEN SAINTS AND SAGES

The esoteric traditions agree on another, related viewpoint: that not all who dwell on earth are still learning lessons. That is, some individuals that we encounter may have completed all their lessons, but exist in our world solely to serve as teachers and guides for others. In Buddhism, such enlightened souls are known as Bodhisattvas, who are said to have delayed their own entrance into nirvana in order to help those needing direction and comfort.

For instance, we are told that Buddha used to sit by the gates of the city and beg for food. He ate only what people gave him. There he was, a fully enlightened being, and yet he sat like a beggar on a busy thoroughfare. How many of the thousands who passed by him were discerning enough to recognize him?

In Kabbalah and Sufism, the mystic branches of Judaism and Islam respectively, virtually the identical notion is expounded. One of the oldest and most profound Jewish legends is that of the thirty-six hidden just men, known in Yiddish as the *Lamed-vovniks* (*lamed-vov* means "thirty-six" in Hebrew). Tradition has taught that in every generation, the world itself is sustained by these secret saints. The Talmud evocatively declared nearly fifteen hundred years ago that these exalted personages "daily receive the Divine Countenance."

Some tales that have come down through the centuries recount that each of these holy figures knows the identity of all the others. In this way, they form a hidden network—a cabal—that spans the continents. In other stories, it is said that members are not even aware of their own individual exalted roles, let alone that of their peers. But common to all variants of this legend, across several spiritual traditions, is that these saints are outwardly quite ordinary, often engaged in the most mundane occupations—as cobblers or water carriers. Or, perhaps in our own time, as raggedy car wash workers or disheveled women selling pretzels and bagels on the street.

We may never be able to prove that this concept is true. But more important for our everyday lives, I believe, is that if we act as if it were true—"Treat everyone you meet as if they were one of the Lamed-Vov" is an old Jewish saying—we will behave very differently toward others. We will cease responding to people on the basis of society's materialistic definitions of success and worth, but rather as intrinsically divine figures. In so doing, we also respect and honor our own self-worth.

## *Identifying Hidden Saints: An Exercise*

In this exercise, think back over the course of your life and identify those people who, through the kindness, simplicity, and quiet serenity displayed to you and others, may have been secret Bodhisattvas or Lamed-vovniks. Focus on your present circumstances and look for possibilities. Remember that flamboyance has never been the style of secret saints; you may therefore have to stimulate your memory and awareness a bit. You may not be able to list all thirty-six yet, but name as many as you can.

You may also wish to assume that, at all times, there is at least one hidden saint secretly operating in your life. If so, who is he or she right now?

# 11

# Embracing Nothing

*If you love something, set it free.*
*If it comes back, it's yours.*
*If it doesn't, it never way.*
Anonymous

It is an unfortunate and dismaying fact that many people become acutely bored when they have nothing to do. Others become extremely anxious. As a psychiatrist, I have seen many patients whose fear of boredom or anxiety is a ceaseless, driving force in how they organize their days. They tend to be conscientious and hard working, but take on more responsibilities and commitments than they can comfortably handle. As a result, they are constantly rushing to get things done and always have many pressing matters that require their immediate attention.

Does this description sound familiar? Typically these individuals are completely unaware of their underlying fear of boredom or anxiety. Indeed, they are likely to complain sincerely about their hectic schedules and many external pressures. They often proclaim loudly their ardent desire for greater tranquility and rest. They keep promising themselves the wonderful peacefulness of having nothing to do. But not now, of course —someday.

People who have adopted this hurried lifestyle—and in our contemporary urban society, many of us have done so—invariably find ways of evading this promise. Even our cherished, long-awaited vacations are typically packed full of too many things to see or accomplish. If we really find ourselves having "nothing to do" despite our elaborately planned itineraries and schedules, we become anxious. Yet, it is only then that we can catch a glimpse, if we choose to look, of our intense avoidance of "nothingness."

What is transpiring in these situations? I believe that our fear of nothingness relates to, or conceals, a deeper fear of losing control. Although we all experience this worry at times, there are some men and women whose lives are dominated by it. Through personal episodes, they have learned that as long as they have something to do, they can maintain a sense of control. In a curious way, their outlook can remain relatively calm even when they feel overwhelmed by pressures and work load, for on another level they realize that they have set up, and thereby ultimately control, their stressful situation. But when they sense a *lack* of control, even in such relatively benign circumstances as being stuck in traffic or waiting in a bank line, they quickly become frustrated, restless, anxious, and irritable.

Our fears of the unknown, of confronting certain thoughts, of feelings, and of strong inner drives, are all variations on the theme of losing control. Consequently, some people find it more satisfying to be overscheduled and thereby "know" what they will face each day, than to be confronted with the ambiguous gift of unstructured time. Such time leaves space for painful thoughts and feelings or perhaps for sexual, aggressive, and other uncomfortable impulses. In each of these circumstances, "nothing to do" is threatening, because such people experience it as a loss of control. They continually build planned activities and structured time into their day-to-day lives as means of keeping themselves in line.

Many of us are not aware of our anxiety about losing control. For the most part, our dread about the possibility of facing "nothing" looms only as a vague discomfort, a fear that remains nondescript and free-floating. We tend to prize our superorganized lifestyle and our high level of activity as productive and desirable. However, the real issue is not the potential usefulness of these patterns, but rather the underlying fears that have driven us to develop them, so that we no longer have the option of being relaxed and "nonproductive." Our fear of nothing contributes much to our daily ennui, our overall sense of being unfulfilled.

## RECOGNIZING OUR FEAR

Karen, forty-three, sought group therapy because of chronic depression. She was a warm, giving, and potentially vibrant woman who saw herself as the victim of a loveless marriage. She cried when others spoke of their marital happiness and bemoaned the fact that she was miserable with her passive and phobia-ridden husband, Leonard. Karen repeatedly told the group of Leonard's inadequacies, his lack of sexual assertiveness, his timidity in business, his inability to make decisions, his lack of leadership in running their household. "I have to do everything," Karen railed to the group. "If I don't nag him, nothing gets done. I don't want to be like this, but he leaves me no choice. I can't stand it when he lets things go!"

In time, it became clear to all that Karen inadvertently perpetuated the very problems that upset her so much. Though she had accurately described Leonard's passive behavior, she had hidden from herself what she did to encourage these traits in him and how she profited by them.

Karen was constantly on the go, trying to keep matters at home in order and under control. Impatient with Leonard's slowness to act, she did almost everything herself. He once decided to handle the bill paying, but when he made an error in their checkbook account, she took this responsibility away from him. On the few occasions when Leonard mustered enough courage to make a sexual advance, she criticized his lovemaking. Karen frequently pointed out in a derogatory manner mistakes Leonard had made in household decisions. Although experience had taught Karen that such nagging made him lose enthusiasm for his business work, she would consistently nag Leonard about not working enough at the office.

The group began to help Karen focus on her role in this partnership, and the unhealthy needs that her marriage was satisfying. In response, Karen, an only child, spoke of her mother's sudden death when she was eleven and of the subsequent burdens that fell on her, which were aggravated by her father's irresponsibility. "I was eleven chronologically," she commented, "but closer to age six in terms of my maturity. My mother had babied me and done everything for me. And then she suddenly died."

Although Karen had spoken about this issue during several previous group sessions, this was the first time that she was able to connect to her deep feeling of abandonment and her submerged anger at her dead mother for "leaving" the family. Karen also began to verbalize a long-suppressed resentment toward her father for his lack of involvement in the day-to-day running of the household. She cited his neglect in paying bills as a prime example:

> It's not that he didn't have the money. It's just that he never bothered with such things. . . . If I didn't open the mail, he wouldn't even see the bills. Often I came home from school and found the electricity, gas, or telephone shut off. It was frightening not to know what would be turned off next. It was up to me to get things done. I just couldn't depend on him. The only way I could be sure, was to do it myself.

Through interacting with other group members, Karen came to recognize and articulate her fear of not being in control of all situations. For her, control meant doing everything herself, and lack of control meant chaos. In her avowed effort never to let events get out of control again, Karen chose a husband who did not assert himself and who thus allowed, or as she initially saw it, *forced* her to assume control of the household. When she tried following the advice of a previous therapist to *not* perform certain chores purposely, so that Leonard would be forced to do them, she recalled becoming "almost crazy. . . . It drove me up a wall to sit back and not do something. I can't just not do something when I know it has to be done."

Karen eventually realized that her need to *do* things all the time was not limited to relating to her spouse, but involved her overall behavior. She finally saw that as long as she had something to do, she felt in control; therefore, she was always doing something. Leonard's relative inactivity served as a convenient smoke screen to keep her from examining her own fear of losing control.

The case of Heather, thirty-three, is another example of this same problem. Heather had studied dance therapy and taught dance in a local public school system. Her chief complaint was that she had an overriding need to please other people. She succumbed to internal pressure to please others, even though doing so frequently meant abandoning her own needs and interests.

Although Heather resented her tendency always to put herself last, she did not dare to do otherwise. Why? Because, as she recognized, her chief source of self-esteem was a feeling that others appreciated her. She believed that other people would value her only if she continued to do things that pleased them. She described herself in this way: "I have a need to produce, to show something for myself. . . . If I haven't done anything, then I feel like nothing."

Accomplishing things became the measure of Heather's relationships with others, as well as of her sense of self. If she did not produce things, she anticipated that she would not merely be "un-liked," but would actually become "no-thing."

In discussing this fear, Heather recalled two recurring situations in which she had felt like nothing. The first involved her professional work. Due to space limitations, the school in which Heather taught part-time was unable to provide her with a private consulting room. As a result, she had to teach vagabond-style, in different classrooms throughout the school building. "I don't have a space for myself," she lamented. "I would feel good about myself if only I had my own classroom." The second situation involved a psychologist with whom she was leading a psychotherapy group with an emphasis on dance therapy. Heather kept thinking, "Once the psychologist sees the dance techniques that I know, she won't need me anymore and will be able to run the whole group herself. I will have nothing."

In both these cases, it was Heather's reliance on something outside herself that generated her feelings of insecurity. As long as she defined "my space" as some tangible object outside of herself such as a consulting room, the possession of that thing, or its lack, determined the quality of her existence. Similarly, by defining herself in terms of the particular skills she could perform, Heather rendered her self-worth vulnerable to external circumstances. It was when Heather began perceiving that her "space" was within herself, and that she was more than the sum of her professional skills and activities, that she initiated the first major, adult steps to revitalizing her self-worth.

## THE ACTIVITY TRAP

For some people, the activity they pursue must be "meaningful" or "productive." It may even be acceptable for such persons to have brief periods in which they have nothing to do, provided that they spend adequate time performing tasks that they deem worthwhile and important. For example, many housewives feel that they are doing nothing, despite the hard work and responsibility needed to run a household and raise a family. Typically in our work-oriented society, we measure or even define ourselves by what we do for a living ("I am a lawyer," "I am a secretary").

Many people can enjoy themselves only when their activity is aimed at accomplishing a specific goal. They may be satisfied with reading books, taking courses, or engaging in other activities that provide an opportunity to learn, even if the knowledge they are gaining is not immediately applicable to their professions or careers. However, their satisfaction still depends on their involvement with one form of learning or another. Anything potentially enjoyable that lies outside the educational process is dismissed as "a waste of time."

Our almost relentless need to fill our waking hours with something to do has helped build the recreation industry into a multibillion dollar enterprise. Yet often, our recreational activities and vacations leave us unfulfilled, or even depressed. This reaction often results from the feeling that we have not accomplished enough, and therefore cannot feel good about ourselves. In order to enjoy a vacation or recreational activity, we need to justify it on pragmatic grounds: it must recharge us or enhance our productivity when we return to work!

I know of many couples whose marriages would surely be strained should television suddenly disappear from the earth. Although such couples spend a lot of time together, it is usually time spent emotionally distanced from each other. These couples have become so dependent on television to fill their waking hours that they would quickly become anxious and irritable if this activity were gone. There are also couples who invariably arrange to spend the bulk of their free time busily visiting friends or involved in highly structured activities like playing tennis or attending the theatre.

In essence, these couples are seeking to avoid having to be alone together with "nothing to do," for this situation would require dealing with their deadened relationship and their suppressed feelings about themselves and one another.

## WHAT IS NOTHING?

I could cite countless examples of our culture's fear of nothing. We tend to associate the word "nothing" with an emptiness, a void, a vacuum that nature is reputed to abhor. Consequently, we are socialized to regard having nothing, doing nothing, and being nothing as situations to be vigorously avoided. The absurdity and irony of such an attitude toward nothing begins to become clear when we discover that the dreaded word is actually made up of two shorter words: "no" and "thing." "Nothing" means merely *the absence of things.*

A "thing" is defined by Webster as "a tangible object, as distinguished from a concept or quality: any single entity distinct from all others." Thus "nothing" is hardly a void; it is merely the absence of tangible objects. Our fear of "nothing" ultimately reflects the degree of our involvement with the world of the many —to the exclusion of the world of the one.

Our dread of nothing is directly proportional to the extent to which we value things. Moreover, our dread is inversely proportional to our degree of self-worth. To strengthen self-worth, we need to differentiate between a nothing and a void.

After all, an object is tangible only when it impinges on one of our five senses. We hear nothing when a sound is either above or below the frequencies humans can hear; a common example is a dog whistle. We see nothing when light is of a wavelength beyond the spectrum perceived by human vision, ultraviolet light, for example. Similarly, we smell, taste, and feel nothing unless the stimulus is confined to the narrow range detectable by human senses. It is well known that many animals are capable of responding to a wide range of sensory stimuli which they perceive though our human senses tell us that nothing is there.

Our five senses, wondrous as they are, are intrinsically limited and limiting. Like the proverbial blind men, who each grasp a different part of an elephant's voluminous body, we can detect with our senses only a portion of the world around us. Our worship of things is based on clinging to partial perception, as if it were a view of the whole. In contrast, true self-worth is based on the mutual and appropriate balance of things and "no things."

Even within the confines of our five senses, things can often limit our experience of the beauty that surrounds us. For example, most people at one time or another have held up a hand to block the sun's rays from their eyes. Despite its vast brightness, the sun can be blocked from our vision by almost anything that we hold close to our eyes. Similarly, the more we surround ourselves with material objects, the more we block our awareness of *other things* and of *no things*.

An old Jewish tale speaks meaningfully to this point. There was once a rabbi in a small East European town whose synagogue members were mainly poor people. In the same town, there lived one very wealthy man who belonged to the congregation and had been its prime benefactor. Over the years this man had become increasingly miserly and contributed less and less money to charity. Finally, he refused to contribute anything at all for the synagogue's upkeep. Pleas offered by members of the congregation fell on deaf ears.

Distressed about this situation, the rabbi decided to visit the wealthy man at home and talk directly to him. However, with all the rabbi's prestige, knowledge, and logic, he fared no better than had his congregants. The wealthy man obstinately refused to part with any of his savings.

In dismay, the rabbi was about to leave when he suddenly noticed a mirror and had a flash of insight. He called his miserly host over to the mirror, and asked him to gaze into it and describe what he saw. Puzzled, the miser looked into the mirror and replied, "I see myself, of course!"

"Good!" said the rabbi. "Now, please come over to this window and tell me what you see."

The wealthy man approached the window, which faced the town's main street. Even more puzzled, the man answered after a pause, "I see people."

"Exactly!" exclaimed the rabbi. "But do you realize that the mirror and the window are both made of glass? The only difference is that the mirror is coated with silver. When silver gets in the way, all you can see is yourself."

Deeply moved by the rabbi's cogent observation about how silver (or money) can change a person's view of himself and others, the man underwent an immediate change of heart and became generous once more.

## THE TRAP OF AVOIDING FEELINGS

We also deny or denigrate our self-worth by engaging in the *doing* or *withholding* of things to represent our feelings, instead of expressing them directly. For instance, a wife becomes angry at her husband because he does not help clean up after they have entertained guests. Instead of verbalizing her anger, she decides not to cook his favorite meal the following night as she had planned. Or consider the case of a man who is pleased with the excellent service he has received in a restaurant. He does not directly inform the waiter, but instead leaves a munificent tip.

I am not arguing that the things done or withheld in such instances are necessarily inappropriate. Nor am I suggesting that the husband or waiter may not comprehend the underlying message and know the exact feelings intended. Rather, my point is that by allowing things to do our speaking for us, instead of articulating feelings like "I'm angry at you for not helping to clean up," or "thank you for the excellent service tonight," we not only diminish our relations with others, but also lose contact with ourselves. When we permit things to be the sole means through which we express our emotions, we erode the ground in which self-worth can flourish.

By overemphasizing the value of things, we devalue no-thing, yet self-worth ultimately has more to do with intangible aspects inside ourselves than with tangible possessions. All too often, we confuse our self-worth with having something, accomplishing something, or being something significant in the eyes of others. Such attributes can certainly improve our life in many ways, but they actually have little bearing on either developing or strengthening self-worth.

However, I am not saying that possessions, accomplishments, or reputation stand in opposition to self-worth. It is undoubtedly possible to have, do, or be something and still have a strong sense of self-worth, generated independent of these externals. However, having, being, or doing something special often give rise to a false sense of self-worth that, despite its air of authenticity and strength, collapses once the external aspects on which it is based are shaken.

What does this awareness mean in concrete terms? Speaking about her work with thousands of terminally ill persons, Dr. Elizabeth Kübler-Ross has noted:

> [Such work] will help you to a different quality of life. You really begin to be aware that all your titles, or your honorary degrees, or your material things, or what kind of car your neighbor has, are such nonsense, are so totally irrelevant that it's absolutely and totally insignificant. The only thing that counts is what you do with your life and the quality of your love that you are able to give and to share and to receive.

In the same talk, Dr. Kübler-Ross said these words to her audience:

> When you love, give it everything you have got and when you have reached your limit, give it more and forget the pain of it, because as you face your death, it is only the love you have given and received which will count. All the rest, the accomplishments, the struggles, the fights, will be forgotten in your reflection. If you have loved well, then it will have been worth it, and the joy of it will last you until the end. But if you have not, death will always come too soon and be too terrible to face.

In the *Spirit of Zen*, British philosopher Alan Watts expressed similar sentiments in writing about the essence of Buddhism:

> Briefly, this doctrine is that man suffers because of his craving to possess and keep for ever things which are essentially impermanent (19). . . . because life is this elusive and perpetually changing process, every time we think we have really taken possession of something, the truth is that we have completely lost it. All that we possess is our own [fixed] idea about the thing desired. . . . Those who try to possess are in fact possessed. (pp. 58-59)

Changing our primary focus from the world of tangible objects to the world of *no things* opens the door to new possibilities of human experience. It weakens society's pressure that we focus on objects outside ourselves, and instead allows us to reinvest our energy in self-awareness and a capacity to know ourselves in a different way. This shift in attitude helps us develop greater self-intimacy, and consequently, a deeper closeness with others.

Creating time that is free from outside stimuli and making peace with the intense quiet of *no things* aids in the process of recontacting ourselves. In this way, we can develop a stronger sense of self-worth and a greater appreciation for life's inherent beauty and value.

## FINDING MEANING

People most often find meaning in life through simple acts, when nothing special or unusual is going on outwardly—in moments of loving and self-loving, in genuine involvement with others, or in experiencing harmony with nature and all that exists. Over the years, my patients have described such moments in words like these:

> Being alone and quiet; feeling warm about myself.
>
> Kissing my child and feeling the kiss fully.
>
> Being with a good friend, and sharing in silence a kind of contact with each other that is hard to put into words.
>
> Looking up at a starlit sky and feeling a sense of being connected to everything.
>
> Walking home on a snowy winter night. Nothing exciting is happening, but everything seems right.

The common denominator among these descriptions is that no things are at the forefront of the individual's awareness. This allows the person's consciousness to be focused wholly on experiencing the moment and joyful emotions arise, even in apparently commonplace situations.

Fritz Perls, co-founder of Gestalt therapy, often addressed himself to the pattern in which we have become so preoccupied with externals that we lose contact with our own essence. He often cited the example of what he termed "giving one's eyes away." For instance, we attend a party or social gathering, but instead of using our eyes to experience all that is happening around us, we use our eyes to see *what we look like to others.* We do look at others, but while doing so, we are mainly concerned with how we appear to them. Thus, much of what we see becomes a basis for comparing ourselves to someone else.

Similarly, when we participate in recreational activities like tennis, we are sometimes more involved in the impression we are making on others while executing a particular stroke than in feeling the flow of our swing. People who are always caught up in directing their energy outward in this way often feel frustrated and depressed. They generally blame their predicament on a lack of happy experiences, but they actually lack the ability to experience the moments of pleasure they do have. This is not an insurmountable problem. However, overcoming this inability requires contact and space—contact with our own being, and contact with an inner space free of external stimuli.

Although depending on material things can create a significant barrier to strong self-worth, the barrier exists largely within our minds and not in physical reality. Therefore, we generally do not need to become ascetics or hermits to enhance our sense of self-worth. Rather, we must embrace no thing, and alter our attitude and attachment to things—in other words, learn not to measure, define, or limit ourselves by things. We should not value *any thing* above life itself.

In this regard, the worst attitude we can adopt is convincing ourselves that we can't live without a particular thing, experience, or response from others. Instead, we must work to maintain our own center at all times, in dealing with *any*thing and *every*thing outside.

From this centered stance, it is even possible to enhance our self-worth through a relationship to things. Once, while visiting a reconstructed eighteenth-century village, I watched a cooper go through the entire process of making a barrel. He took a hatchet and chopped branches from nearby trees to gather the wood he needed. It was clear that he respected the trees, because he chose the branches with great care. Handling each piece of wood with gentle calmness, he cut and planed each board to fit exactly. It took him most of the day to make a single barrel, but the finished product was both aesthetically pleasing and useful. Certainly, his craftsmanship was not very efficient or practical in terms of our society's demands for mass production. But in terms of self-worth and delight in one's work, it was a very productive endeavor.

Thus, the cooper's self-worth was strengthened by a thing, but did not depend on his having that thing. He was enriched by the process of making the barrel—the actions of chopping, planing, and looking at the finished product. It was the experience of expressing himself in relation to the barrel—and not the end-product of the barrel itself—on which his self-worth rested.

Undoubtedly, our socioeconomic system could not survive if all consumer products were made this way. We must depend on assembly line production to compete as a nation in an international economy. But what about the people who work on assembly lines? What of their need to experience genuine pride in their work? While an individual cooper can look at his barrel as an expression of himself, most factory workers can look only at their impersonal paychecks as expressions and measures of themselves. As a result, their salary takes on an inordinate symbolic significance, and they are further removed from a sense of self-worth. It is hardly a coincidence that alcoholism and drug addiction are commonplace among workers in large factories.

Of course, I am not speaking here only of wooden barrels or assembly-line workers. The problem I am discussing can be applied to most jobs in our modern civilization. Because our work is often depersonalized, it is all the more important for us to make time for no things and learn to value that time.

Of course, there are people who are comfortable doing nothing, and indeed some people prefer doing nothing most of the time. However, spending the majority of our time doing nothing is not a path to greater self-worth. Rather it can lead to and express lethargy and depression, and can be as destructive to self-worth as being a workaholic. If we keep the cooper and the rabbi and his mirror/window in mind, we can begin to find the proper balance of things and no things, a balance that is essential for self-worth.

In spite of our fear of anxiety and boredom, and in spite of our tendency to condemn doing nothing as time wasting, we need to reevaluate this concept. We need to set aside time each day, even if only a few minutes, to do absolutely nothing. During this time, do not meditate. Do not seek insights into human existence and the cosmos. Do not analyze your dreams or write in your journal. Do not listen to music or read. Do not socialize, and definitely do not watch television. Just sit and do absolutely nothing.

In this way, "nothing" can become a potent healing force that stimulates and supports the growth of self-worth.

## *Cultivating Nothing: An Exercise*

The following exercise is best done when you have a lot to accomplish and feel pressured by your environment. However, if performing this exercise under such circumstances makes you feel uncomfortable, then try it during a less hectic time.

Take a few minutes out of your busy day. Sit down, or lie down if possible, and devote time to doing nothing. This is not a session for meditating, doing breathing exercises, engaging in planning, or any other structured activity. You are simply to do nothing.

People in whom this task evokes anxiety or restlessness are often precisely those who can benefit most from it. If you are in this category, know that this exercise's purpose is to help you reach a point where "nothing" is no longer so tension arousing.

If you find that your anxiety persists despite repeated sessions, then before you can comfortably do nothing, you will probably have to do something. The something I recommend has five steps:

1. Perform the exercise of doing nothing, but pay careful attention to your body.

2. Become aware of where in your body you are experiencing tension and of the distinct physical sensations you feel there.

3. Allow yourself to stay with these sensations despite their possible unpleasantness. Ordinarily, you would seek to eliminate such sensations, but the objective here is to accept them as fully as you can.

4. If the unpleasantness continues, take the initiative and make these sensations stronger. That is, instead of resisting, go with them and amplify them.

5. As you follow these steps, you will probably notice that the initially unpleasant physical sensations either vanish or change into some other sensations. If they

disappear, so probably will the tension, and you will be able to spend the remainder of the allotted time comfortably doing nothing. If the sensations shift in form or location, follow the preceding steps with each new sensation.

When successfully carried out, these steps will enhance your contact with your body and feelings, crucial ingredients for strengthening self-worth. You may also gain valuable insights into what your fear of *nothing* is really about. However, should repeated attempts yield little or no reduction in anxiety, I recommend that you discontinue the exercise and consider consulting a therapist or spiritual advisor if you wish to embrace nothing.

# 12

# A Time for Healing

*To everything there is a season and a time for every purpose under heaven.*

Ecclesiastes

I began this book by pointing out that in my work with patients suffering from a wide range of illnesses, I became aware that many lacked the vital inner resource of self-worth. I then highlighted a variety of important concepts and practical techniques for developing and enhancing self-worth. In this final chapter, I explore the direct relationship between self-worth and healing.

After many years of medical practice, I have come to realize that a lack of self-worth is integral to the process of getting sick and staying sick. I now see that a major part of any healing treatment is the enhancement of self-worth. I believe that when people become ill, the particular illness, whatever its specific type, manifests on every level of their being. What we doctors see when we examine a sick person depends on what level of the patient's being we look at and how sophisticated we are in accurately diagnosing the sources of the problem.

For example, if we choose to examine a person from a physical viewpoint, what we see is body, and we can detect an illness's manifestation on a body level. If we decide to examine the same individual from a psychological viewpoint, then what we see is mind, and we can note the manifestation of that same illness on a mental level. Should we look biochemically, we can see evidence of a metabolic disturbance, and should we look energetically, we can observe energy imbalances. Similarly, if we look at the same individual from a spiritual viewpoint, we will see the manifestation of the illness on a spiritual level. Therefore, it is not really a question of trying to determine the particular level of a person's illness (Is it a physical problem? A mental problem? A nutritional or metabolic problem?), because illness does not occur only on one level. When disease exists, it permeates the organism.

Furthermore, I am convinced that illness originates at the higher aspects of consciousness and filters down to our physical body. When we lose touch with our center, especially the spiritual and energetic aspects of our being, we create an imbalance that exposes us to illness. Only after that happens do such external causes as bacteria and situational stress trigger symptoms of physical illness. It is crucial to understand that the bacteria or stressful episode is not the primary cause of the disease.

At precisely this point in our discussion, the issue of self-worth enters the picture—not because self-worth is itself the key factor in illness and health, but because our degree of self-worth is a direct measure of our centeredness, our ability to love ourselves and others. Love is, in my opinion, the most potent healing force we possess. Generally, when we begin to lose connection with ourselves, with our capacity to love, and with the oneness of the universe, we also lose connection with our self-worth, and our susceptibility to disease increases. A low sense of self-worth is a significant (though not by itself sufficient) factor in the development of illness. For this reason, developing a strong sense of self-worth helps protect us against a variety of ailments. Similarly, strengthening the self-worth of people who are currently sick can facilitate their recovery. In this way, we can all aid in healing ourselves and others.

## VARIETIES OF HEALING

Just as there are many kinds of sick people in this world, there are many types of healing: a surgeon's knife or antibiotic prescription; a healer's hands; a mother's kiss or a friend's affectionate greeting; timeless words of Scripture or heartfelt prayer. Healing initiated at any level of our being—whether biochemical, mental, energetic or spiritual—affects our entire organism. In general, I feel, intervention aimed at the higher aspects of our being addresses more directly the root cause of our distress, whereas intervention at the lower levels deals predominantly with symptoms. Nevertheless, we need not always reach to the highest levels of being in order to spur the healing process. Sometimes, a band-aid is enough.

Even more important for us to realize is that there are no perfect healers. And that is all right, because there are no perfect patients. No matter what the healer's stage of growth—and we are all qualified to use the title healer—there are sick people who need to be healed at that level and who might not respond to healing directed at other levels of their being. Even great religious healers whose miraculous cures were recorded in the Bible did not heal all people in the same way. For some supplicants, a healer recommended a physical treatment; for others, a healer conducted a laying on of hands. For still others, a word was sufficient. These ancient healers knew the importance of treating each individual as unique.

Like every other power, healing can also be used as a negative force. An attempt at healing can do harm as well as good. To know *what* to heal and when *not* to heal, particularly when the healing involves eliminating symptoms, is as important as knowing *how* to heal. To illustrate these principles, I offer the following cases. They are drawn from my experience as a psychiatrist in the United States Air Force.

Oliver, nineteen, was an unmarried airman who complained to me of being afraid of heights two weeks before he was scheduled to leave for a special paratrooper course for which he had volunteered a few months earlier. He explained that as the time to begin the course was drawing closer, his anxiety was mounting. He asked me to help him overcome his fear of heights.

In many respects, Oliver seemed like an excellent candidate for a behavior therapy desensitization program. This form of treatment is very successful in enabling people to overcome phobias through relaxation and imagery. The treatment is usually completed in a relatively short period of time. However, when I analyzed Oliver's life history from a psychodynamic viewpoint, it became clear that his acrophobia was actually a "cover" for a different and more significant conflict.

Oliver had experienced considerable difficulty getting along with his parents, especially in his adolescence. About a year before coming to see me for psychiatric treatment, he had become engaged to a sixteen-year-old girl, Mary-Ann. She was experiencing similar emotional problems with her own parents. Oliver was conscious of feeling that by marrying Mary-Ann, he would be rescuing her, much as he had hoped that someone could have rescued him from strife with his parents.

Both Oliver's and Mary-Ann's parents were firmly opposed to the youthful marriage and listed many realistic obstacles that stood in the way of its success. However, they agreed that once these obstacles were removed, Oliver and Mary-Ann could get married. At the time of my first session with the young airman, every obstacle had been removed except for a financial one. Oliver could not support a wife on an airman's salary. However, by joining a paratrooper unit, he would get a substantial salary increase, and the last barrier to his marriage would be eliminated.

Oliver himself had not seen the connection between deciding to join the paratroopers and his impending marriage. As I worked with Oliver, it became clear to both of us that his major concern was not really fear of heights, but his ambivalence about whether or not to marry.

Oliver knew that if he completed the paratrooping course, he would be obligated to get married. However, he was not sure if he really wanted to be married at the beginning of his adult life. As long as external obstacles to the marriage existed, he could tell himself and proclaim to others his great desire to marry Mary-Ann. But in his ambivalence, Oliver fell back on his longstanding fear of heights to avoid making a final decision about the marriage.

When Oliver asked me, "Should I go through with the paratrooping course even though I have a fear of heights?" he was also asking, "Should I go through with the marriage even though I have doubts about it?" I saw that he actually hoped that his fear of heights could not be cured, and that he would fail the paratrooping course. In this way, he could still believe that only financial difficulties prevented him from getting married.

After we discussed these issues, Oliver was able to separate his fear of heights from his ambivalence about marriage. He understood that earning more money did not, in fact, obligate him to marry Mary-Ann. When I offered Oliver a course of behavior therapy to overcome his acrophobia, he insisted that he felt confident of conquering his fear of heights on his own, and turned down the offer.

Had Oliver undergone a course of behavior therapy to combat his acrophobia, it likely would have failed. However, had such therapy been effective, his marital anxieties might never have been brought to light. Such healing might have been a curse in disguise, propelling Oliver into a hasty marriage that might have been more detrimental to his life in the long run than his fear of heights.

The second case I would like to discuss is that of Elsie, sixty, a black woman who worked as a civilian employee for the Air Force, ironing clothes at the base laundry. Elsie had burned her right hand severely in an accident with an ironing machine. Over a period of several months, she underwent a series of surgical procedures aimed at restoring normal function and appearance to her hand. Her surgeons were pleased with their work from a technical viewpoint, but Elsie remained totally unable to use her hand. The neurologist and neurosurgeon who consulted on the case could find no physical explanation for her paralysis.

Finally, Elsie's doctors requested a psychiatric consultation, and I became part of the team. I found Elsie to be a soft-spoken, pleasant, and somewhat obese woman, who was awed but simultaneously delighted by all the medical attention being showered upon her. She had a borderline I.Q., no insight concerning her condition, and no inclination or motivation to commit herself to any form of psychotherapy.

Elsie told me that she had been born into a poor family in the South, and had lived with poverty and racial discrimination all of her life. Until her accident, she had worked hard every single day since she was a teenager. Now at the age of sixty, she was not only employed in a hot, uncomfortable, steam-filled room, but she returned from work each day to a house filled with boisterous grandchildren, whom she was raising with only part-time and inconsistent help from her own daughters. Essentially, Elsie did all the shopping, cooking, cleaning, and other domestic chores for the household. It was an exhausting way of life, but one that Elsie had never even questioned until the accident.

Since Elsie had not worked at the base long enough to earn a pension and soon faced mandatory retirement, she worried about her future. However, since she was now unable to use her right hand, Elsie did not have to work at all, because she was receiving money from disability payments. She knew that if the disability was found to be permanent, she would get such compensation for the rest of her life. Faced with no other alternative, her daughters and grandchildren had gradually taken over almost all of the workload at home. Elsie readily acknowledged to me, "Since I hurt that old hand, I've never had it so good in all my life!"

What would happen if Elsie regained use of her hand? Certainly, she would lose her disability payments and have to return to the sweaty ironing room at the base laundry. In a few years, she would face retirement with no pension, only Social Security.

She also knew that if she were well, the old patterns at home would be reestablished. Although Elsie insisted that she wanted to regain the use of her hand, deeper portions of her being were speaking more firmly through the continuing paralysis.

Assuming that I did have the psychiatric know-how, would restoring function to Elsie's hand really have been a healing act? I chose not to try to heal her. I stated to the military review board that her condition appeared intractable, and recommended that her medical disability be continued.

## Symptoms are Gifts

There are times, usually clearer to discern in retrospect, when we may actually need to be ill and our symptoms are misunderstood gifts. An illness, for example a cold, may be an important message that we need to slow down and take it easy for a while. I have found that the premature removal of a mild fever or sore throat can inadvertently cause us to ignore such messages. If we do not get the physical rest necessitated by a mild illness, we may eventually risk a considerably more serious medical problem. Symptoms can thus be friends that arise to protect us from what we consider, either consciously or unconsciously, a greater evil. The cases of airman Oliver and his fear of heights and Elsie and her paralyzed hand illustrate this point clearly.

Once we realize that symptoms can be helpful, we must ask: Should a doctor force healing on someone who does not want to be healed? Or rather, does the true healer understand that healing may in fact lie within the process of being ill and perhaps even within the process of dying?

I have learned again and again in my work that I am most helpful during those precious times when I am centered and attuned to the oneness that binds the patient and myself. I benefit as much from these moments of peak effectiveness as does the patient. In fact, in such interaction the roles of physician and patient, healer and healee disappear. We are simply two people engaged in a process of mutual healing and growth.

# Epilogue

In this book, we find the model of an interconnected system where the violation or neglect of any one aspect of being damages the whole. This model is a way of perceiving both the universal and the individual. We understand that when any one species of life becomes extinct, the entire chain of life is compromised. So too for the individual. When we disown feelings because of learned shame, when we betray our bodies with toxic substances, when we evaluate who we are by what we own, we damage every aspect of the self. The results are reflected in a society filled with violence, addiction, and despair.

My husband writes, "When we begin to lose connection with ourselves, with our capacity to love, and with the oneness of the universe, we also lose connection with our self-worth . . ." He tells us that self-worth is an innate part of our humanness, but it must be nurtured if it is to remain vital. As soon as we reject or deny any part of our life energy, we diminish our aliveness and our sense of self-worth along with it.

Scientific and medical research confirms daily that there is a profound connection between mind, body, and spirit, a powerful ongoing interaction between our health, both physical and psychological, and our thinking. Personal beliefs can extend our capacities or they can cripple us. How we nurture or neglect our bodies has a direct impact on our energy for living creative and fulfilling lives. As we learn to integrate all parts of self in a compassionate way, we free energy previously used to negate, censor, and condemn aspects of our experience. Our possibilities expand beyond the limits we have accepted as reality and with them, our capacity for loving action.

And so, in this book, we are taught methods of honoring the human experience on all levels, respecting the life process as it unfolds in the self and the universal. To stay connected with that life process is no easy task in a world that can be fragmented, violent, and dehumanizing. Of course we lose our balance in the process of negotiating life. Out of our anxiety and pain, we devalue ourselves and hurt those around us. What David offers us is a way back to center. We must consciously and willfully incorporate practices and belief systems that teach the value of joy *and* pain, words *and* silence, action *and* stillness.

As he describes in his chapter on meditation, "The mother must find a way through love and gentleness to coax the child . . . without making the child feel ashamed or guilty . . . back to the path." The methods presented in this book give us tools to lovingly and gently get ourselves back on the path. Life then becomes a movement meditation in which we create and recreate our balance in an unbalanced world.

Lynn G. Sheinkin

# Bibliography


Airola, Paavo. *How to Get Well.* Phoenix, AZ: Health Plus Publishers, 1974.

Bach, Richard. *Illusions: The Adventures of a Reluctant Messiah.* New York: Delacorte, 1977.

Bates, William. *The Bates Method for Better Eyesight Without Glasses.* New York: Holt, Rinehart & Winston, 1940, 1943.

Benson, Herbert, and Klipper, Miriam. *The Relaxation Response.* New York: Avon, 1976.

Da, Liu. *T'ai Chi Ch'uan and I Ching: A Choreography of Body and Mind.* New York: Harper & Row, 1978.

Durckheim, Karlfried. *Hara: The Vital Center of Man.* London: George Allen and Unwin, 1962, 1989.

Govinda, Lama Anagarika. *Creative Meditation and Multi-Dimensional Consciousness.* Wheaton, IL: Theosophical Publishing House, Quest, 1986, 1990.

Herrigel, Eugen. *Zen in the Art of Archery.* New York: Random House, 1989.

Heschel, Abraham. *Between God and Man, an Interpretation of Judaism.* New York: Macmillan, Free Press, 1965.

Huang, Al. *Embrace Tiger, Return to Mountain.* Berkeley, CA: Celestial Arts, 1973, 1987.

Ichazo, Oscar. *Master Level Exercise: Psycho-Calisthenics.* New York: Sequoia NYC, 1986.

Keleman, Stanley, *Sexuality, Self, and Survival.* San Francisco: Lodestar Press, 1971.

Kilner, Walter J. *The Human Aura.* Secaucus, NJ: Carol Publishing Group, Citadel, 1977.

Kübler-Ross, Dr. Elizabeth. From an unpublished tape in the author's personal collection.

Kunkel, Fritz, and Dickerson, Roy E. *How Character Develops.* New York: Charles Scribner's Sons, 1940.

Lecomte duNouy, Pierre. *Human Destiny.* New York: Longman's Green & Co., 1947.

Leonard, George. *The Ultimate Athlete: Re-Visioning Sports, Physical Education, and the Body.* New York: Viking, 1975.

Lindbergh, Charles. *The Spirit of St. Louis.* New York: Charles Scribner's Sons, 1953.

Lowen, Dr. Alexander. *Pleasure: A Creative Approach to Life.* New York: Penguin, 1975.

_________. *The Way to Vibrant Health: A Manual of Bioenergetic Exercises.* New York: Harper & Row, 1977.

Luzzatto, Rabbi Moses C. *The Way of God.* New York: Feldheim Publishers, 1978.

Moody, Raymond. *Life after Life: The Investigation of a Phenomenon, Survival of Bodily Death.* New York: Walker & Co., 1988.

Ott, John. *Health & Light.* Greenwich, CT: Devin, 1988.

Perls, Fritz. *Gestalt Therapy Verbatim.* New York: Bantam, 1972.

Pike, Geoff. *The Power of Chi.* New York: Bell, 1980.

Richards, M. C., *Centering: In Poetry, Pottery, & the Person.* Middletown, CT: Wesleyan University Press, 1964.

Sheinkin, David. *Path of the Kabbalah.* New York: Paragon, 1986.

_________, Schachter, Michael, and Hutton, Richard. *Food, Mind and Mood.* New York: Warner, 1987.

Smith, David. *The East West Exercise Book.* New York: McGraw Hill, 1976.

Smith, Philip. *Total Breathing.* New York: McGraw Hill, 1980.

Speads, Carola. *Ways to Better Breathing.* Great Neck, NY: F. Morrow, 1986.

Tohei, Koichi. *KI Breathing Methods.* H.Q. Japan: KI NO Kenkyukai, 1975.

_________. *Aikido in Daily Life.* Tokyo, Japan: Rikugei Publishing House, 1966.

Thie, John F. *Touch for Health.* Pasadena, CA: DeVorss & Co., 1973, 1979.
Volin, Michael. *Challenging the Years.* New York: Harper & Row, 1979.
Watts, Alan. *The Spirit of Zen: A Way of Life, Work, & Art in the Far East.* New York: Grove, 1987.
Yogi Ramacharaka. *Science of Breath.* Fowler & Co., 1960.

# Index for Exercises

QUEST BOOKS
are published by
The Theosophical Society in America,
Wheaton, Illinois 60189-0270,
a branch of a world organization
dedicated to the promotion of the unity of
humanity and the encouragement of the study of
religion, philosophy, and science, to the end that
we may better understand ourselves and our place in
the universe. The Society stands for complete
freedom of individual search and belief.
In the Classics Series well-known
theosophical works are made
available in popular editions.
For more information
write or call.
1-708-668-1571